Civilized Oppression

For you, Eva;
Blessings, Amorylucha,
Rafael

Civilized Oppression

J. Harvey

ROWMAN & LITTLEFIELD PUBLISHERS, INC.
Lanham • Boulder • New York • Oxford

ROWMAN & LITTLEFIELD PUBLISHERS, INC.

Published in the United States of America
by Rowman & Littlefield Publishers, Inc.
4720 Boston Way, Lanham, Maryland 20706
http://www.rowmanlittlefield.com

12 Hid's Copse Road
Cumnor Hill, Oxford OX2 9JJ, England

British Library Cataloguing in Publication Information Available

Library of Congress Cataloging-in-Publication Data

Harvey, Jean, 1955–
    Civilized oppression / J. Harvey.
      p.   cm.
    Includes bibliographical references and index.
    ISBN 0-8476-9274-4 (cloth : alk. paper). — ISBN 0-8476-9275-2
  (pbk : alk. paper)
    1. Oppression (Psychology) 2. Discrimination. I. Title.
  HM1266.H37   1999
  305—dc21   99-35063
                                                            CIP

Printed in the United States of America

♾ ™ The paper used in this publication meets the minimum requirements of
American National Standard for Information Sciences—Permanence of Paper for
Printed Library Materials, ANSI/NISO Z39.48–1992.

"It is evil to assent actively or passively to evil as its instrument, as its observer or as its victim."

—Rudolf Vrba with Alan Bestic, *I Cannot Forgive*

Contents

Acknowledgments

Some chapters contain material from earlier publications. Passages from the following articles appear in the chapters cited: "Humor as Social Act: Ethical Issues," *The Journal of Value Inquiry* 29, no. 1 (March 1995): 19–30, in chapter 1, with kind permission from Kluwer Academic Publishers; "Social Privilege and Moral Subordination," forthcoming in the *Journal of Social Philosophy*, in chapters 3 and 6, with kind permission of Blackwell Publishers; "Oppression, Moral Abandonment, and the Role of Protest," the *Journal of Social Philosophy* 27, no. 1 (Spring 1996): 156–71, in chapter 4, and "Categorizing and Uncovering 'Blaming the Victim' Incidents," the *Journal of Social Philosophy* 26, no. 2 (Fall 1995): 46–65, in chapter 5, both with kind permission of the *Journal of Social Philosophy*; "Justice Theory and Oppression," forthcoming in the *Canadian Journal of Philosophy*, in chapter 6, with kind permission of the *Canadian Journal of Philosophy*; "The Emerging Practice of Institutional Apologies," *The International Journal of Applied Philosophy* 9, no. 2 (Winter/Spring 1995): 57–65, in chapter 7, with kind permission of *The International Journal of Applied Philosophy*. The book's epigraph is from Rudolf Vrba with Alan Bestic, *I Cannot Forgive* (Vancouver: Regent College Publishing, 1997), and is printed with kind permission of the publisher.

Chapter 1

Concealed Weapons

When we think of oppression, we think of police abducting people in the middle of the night, people being tortured, lynched, or arbitrarily imprisoned, queues of waiting voters being shot, homes burned to the ground, children working chained to cellar walls, dissident writers confined to psychiatric wards or labor camps. We think of systematic brutality, terror, and evil on a scale that shocks. Much of it may go on behind locked doors, but at least it is the kind of evil that should be recognizable as evil by those who do observe it.

Such brutality may be legalized or not, but if we think further about oppression, we may think of cases where the law is used to oppress, but in less obviously violent ways. In various times and places laws have prohibited women from voting, workers from forming unions, married women from continuing in their employment, and religious minorities from holding government office. Other laws have required some people to sit at the back of buses, members of ethnic minorities to carry special identification or hand over their business assets to the government, and children to regularly recite a state-imposed set of prayers. There are penalties if the laws are broken, and there can be violence lurking behind either prohibitive or requirement laws, but still, there may be little violence involved if the laws are complied with.

It is harder still to become aware of what I call "civilized oppression," that involves neither physical violence nor the use of law. Yet these subtle forms are by far the most prevalent in Western industrialized societies. This work will focus on issues that are common to such subtle oppression in several different contexts (such as racism, classism, and sexism), rather than issues specific to just one context. Not everything can be done in any one book, so the goals are the most foundational ones: to analyze what is involved in such oppression, to make such oppression far more recognizable, and to uncover the underlying principles that account for its immorality. It is a different kind of challenge to deal with violent and barbarous

1

oppression (as in the searching and powerful analysis to be found in Laurence Thomas's *Vessels of Evil*[1]).

Analyzing what is involved in civilized oppression includes analyzing the kinds of mechanisms used, the power relations at work, the systems controlling perceptions and information, the kinds of harms inflicted on the victims, and the reasons why this oppression is so hard to see even by contributing agents. Some of the elements lack any familiar description, and in several places an appropriate concept has to be developed before points can be captured.

The second goal—*to make civilized oppression more recognizable*—is one I have in mind throughout the work. Analyzing the various components can reveal what is hiding in full view. It can also uncover subtle reasons why participants, bystanders, and sometimes victims remain unaware of some relationship matters that deeply affect their lives.

The diagnosis of what is morally objectionable about civilized oppression leads to more foundational levels of moral theory. It is a central claim of this book that relationships themselves, rather than obvious tangible harms, lie at the heart of civilized oppression, and although distortions there tend to result in blatant harms like economic deprivation or even physical attack, I will argue that the relationships can be morally unsound in an ongoing way without any such straightforward tangible harms.

These relationships block the exercise of certain basic moral rights and obligations that attach to membership in the moral community and reflect the proper functioning of the community. I will set out some of the *underlying principles* which define these rights and obligations and which *account for the immorality of civilized oppression*. These principles illuminate the ways in which inappropriate relationships exclude and isolate the victims. When vulnerable people are trapped in networks of such relationships, they undergo "moral subordination," the central component of civilized oppression.

A SENSE OF HUMOR

We can begin this whole inquiry by looking at one familiar aspect of social life. We will find that morally disturbing phenomena can be buried in day-to-day incidents of no obvious significance. To illustrate, I will consider the social functioning of humor, since even a brief exploration that takes us below the surface will reveal some of the basic insights relevant to nonviolent oppression.

Having a sense of humor is a highly prized personal attribute in Western societies in these times. The desirability of humor seems so obvious we may not think about justifying this belief. Yet humor, or at least humor expressed in hearty laughter, has been frowned upon by more than one notable thinker. Plato, for example, insists that "We must not allow poets to describe men of worth being overcome by [laughter]; still less should Homer speak of the gods giving way to 'unquenchable laughter'. . . ."[2] The instruction is given as one of his guidelines on education. Presumably Plato is concerned with the demeaning portrayal of "men of worth," and perhaps also concerned that students reading the poetry will be encouraged to indulge in such laughter themselves. Either way, hearty laughter is clearly undesirable.

The most frequent reasons for this claim are that loud laughter signals a lack of intelligence, a lack of self-control, or is aesthetically distasteful.[3] The stereotype associating hearty laughter with a lack of intelligence has existed for a surprisingly long time, given how unfounded it is. Oliver Goldsmith writes of "the loud laugh that spoke the vacant mind."[4] As for aesthetic revulsion toward laughter, it would be hard to find a more delightful example than in the writings of the Fourth Earl of Chesterfield. He combines an aesthetic objection with clear hints about a lack of intelligence. In letters of advice to his son, he declares: "Frequent and loud laughter is the characteristic of folly and ill manners; it is the manner in which the mob express their silly joy at silly things, and they call it being merry. In my mind there is nothing so illiberal and so ill-bred as audible laughter."[5] For this reason, "a man of parts and fashion is . . . only seen to smile, but never heard to laugh."[6] And to show that he follows his own admonitions, he at one point proudly declares, "I am sure that since I had full use of my reason, nobody has ever heard me laugh."[7]

In more recent times the general attitude toward humor and laughter has been very different. People are expected both to initiate and appreciate humor, and anyone who does not, anyone "with no sense of humor," will pay a price for it. As the essayist Frank Moore Colby points out, people "will confess to treason, murder, arson, false teeth, or a wig. How many of them will own up to a lack of humor?"[8] Yet although so highly valued, humor remains one of the few socially acceptable forms of attack on the already disadvantaged, and in ways that are often not seen.

The trouble starts when we ask why humor is so desirable. The reasons usually refer to a kind of character and an approach to life, both considered desirable. People with a sense of humor are more enjoyable as company. We hear that they have "a sense of proportion" about their own situations. They can laugh at themselves, and have a flexible, rather than dogmatic, approach to life. And all of these are given as clearly preferable to their contraries.

Yet these accounts of the value of humor often embody two major problems. The first I call "the individual-based approach." The second is the focusing on socially privileged people while drawing very general conclusions. Both of these problems are illustrated in John Morreall's recent and vivid defense of the value of humor.[9] He contrasts a person with a sense of humor with "a serious person," who is "solemn and anxious," whereas the person with a sense of humor is "more relaxed, less disappointed by failure, and in general more cheerful."[10] He explains that:

> The nonpractical stance in humor, along with its openness to novelty in experience, keeps us from anxiety. . . . With a sense of humor we are especially well equipped to face new situations, and even failure, with interest, since humor is based on novelty and incongruity, on having one's expectations violated. The distance in humor, too, gives us a measure of objectivity in looking at ourselves. . . . Hence we are less egocentric and more realistic in our view of the world. We are more humble in moments of success, less defeated in times of trouble, and in general, more accepting of things the way they are.[11]

I will argue that because of the two problems, much of this is dangerously misleading.

THE INDIVIDUAL-BASED APPROACH

The individual-based approach to humor assesses its value in terms of the individual's character and approach to life. For example, a sense of humor, claims Morreall, enables the individual to handle failure well—no other person is mentioned in reference to "failure" here. It will also enable the person to be "objective" and is a sign that the person has self-esteem without, however, being egocentric.

But the individual-based approach to humor is in general inappropriate. The expressing of a sense of humor is typically a social act, and how others are involved is crucial. Analyzing these social acts alters the very perception of what humor is when it is at work, and a number of moral issues begin to emerge.

Intentional humor can involve three sets of players: the initiator, the "audience," and the subject of the humor. The initiator is the *primary agent* in the act of humor. By the *subject* of the humor, say, of a joke, I mean the person the joke is about. The others present I have referred to as "the audience," but this is really a misnomer. A peculiar feature of acts of humor is that there is not much room for genuine bystanders. The telling of a joke calls for a response. As Henri Bergson notes, "laughter appears to stand in need of an echo."[12] To laugh at the joke is to be involved. Those who do are participants who have aligned themselves with the joke-teller. They have become *secondary agents* in the act of humor. In speaking of malicious humor, the playwright Sheridan writes: "To smile at the jest which places a thorn in another's breast, is to become a principal in the mischief."[13] If, on the other hand, they comprehend the joke but do not laugh or even smile, this too is a response. It is a message of disassociation. The call for a response is answered, although not in the way the joke-teller expects. Either way the listeners have cast their votes. Perhaps the only person who remains clearly a bystander is someone who cannot follow the joke—and does not conceal the fact.

Those present who are neither initiator nor subject of the joke play a vital role in an act of humor. In a sense they must be "on board" if the joke is to succeed. These secondary agents give weight to the act by endorsing it.

These points might not be morally important except for one additional empirical fact: it is not a random matter who tends to initiate humor or who can typically rely on secondary agent endorsement. Humor is inherently a risky business, since it succeeds only if those present respond in the desired way. In mixed groups where some people are highly vulnerable in various ways and others are extremely secure, it is not an accident that humor tends to be initiated by the secure. It is also not an accident that the readiness of others to become secondary agents increases in proportion to the security and power of the joke's initiator. When Caligula tells a joke, people laugh.

When the joke is actually about someone present, then the pattern is even more emphasized. The trend is for the joke-teller to be as powerful— and often more powerful—than the subject of the joke.

We are surely all aware of these trends. As Oliver Goldsmith writes, "the jests of the rich are ever successful."[14] As well as calling upon our daily observations, field studies and experiments have repeatedly confirmed that this pattern holds when the subject of the joke is present.[15] In some of the studies of joking in the workplace, researchers failed to record a single instance where a relatively vulnerable employee told a joke about a more powerful person in the presence of that person. The subject of the joke had either less power than the joke-teller, or at most equal power, so the pattern of joke-telling was asymmetrical in this respect. These empirical facts are easily explained. Where the relative positions of power differ, there are obvious prudential reasons for these trends. The game of humor is not played on a level field—especially when the subject of the humor is present.

People differ with respect to all kinds of factors that bring with them power and security: their financial situation, health, intelligence, good looks, kind of home, ethnic origin, sex, employment status. Some of these, such as serious differences in health, involve a difference in natural resources, like the major loss of energy that accompanies many illnesses.

Others, like the relevance of employment status, good looks, or being female or male, involve constructed social status differences. Where people have much the same power, I will refer to them as "peers." Where they differ significantly I will speak of "nonpeers"—a useful distinction I will say more about later, and one I will call upon throughout the book.

THE RELEVANCE OF NONPEER RELATIONSHIPS

If all the people involved are peers, then much of the moral danger involved in an act of humor is avoided. This is not because nothing can go wrong, but because if it does, there is some chance of a direct response from the person who finds it objectionable. The situation is quite different if the people involved are nonpeers.

If the manager of a small firm is hosting an annual party for the personnel, including, say, the one secretary, then the manager and the secretary are nonpeers in this social situation. The manager is the host and the host is "in charge." The manager is hosting this party as manager, so some of the power of this role is involved. Suppose also that the manager is one of an exclusively male management team, while the employees are all women. Then there is a gender-related status difference. And the party is taking place at the manager's house, which is his territory. In addition, a difference in financial resources may be clearly visible. A person making a very modest wage and living in barely adequate accomodation can easily feel overwhelmed and out of place in a home filled with luxury. For these reasons the manager may have even more power here than at the office.

On prudential grounds the secretary is vulnerable to being induced to laugh at any joke of the manager's. In addition, her vulnerability makes it more likely that she, rather than the manager, will be the subject of a joke. People at the party may not joke about anyone present, but if they do, they are more likely, again for prudential reasons, to pick as the subject someone who does not have power over them, and either make that person the subject of a personal joke or make a joke about a group of subjects in some way represented by that person, say, a joke about female secretaries. This in itself does not guarantee that the joke about the secretary—the content of the joke—is morally unacceptable, but it does mean that she may have no safe recourse if it is.

An adequate assessment of the value of humor cannot be undertaken without reflecting on these social dimensions. The role of nonpeer relationships and the basic appeal of prudence reveal the potential for more moral danger than first meets the eye, and it is danger that is unlikely to be revealed on an individual-based approach.

THE PERSPECTIVE OF THE SOCIALLY PRIVILEGED

My second objection to many accounts of the desirability of humor is the focus on the privileged members of society. We hear, for example, of robust egos benefitting from a bit of deflating, of successes which humor will enable the person to handle with more modesty, of being less defeated in times of trouble.[16] Roughly the value of humor lies in "bringing everything down to size." This is an assessment of the value of humor strictly from "the winners' circle."

Many who live a life that has for a long time been constrained and oppressed may see in all this little that constitutes good reasons for humor's overall desirability. There may be few robust egos here, given that a strong ego thrives in an atmosphere of fulfillment, recognition, and mutual respect. Someone living in poverty in an inner city ghetto may never know the value of humor in handling success with becoming modesty. Doing well in some way is one thing, but success involves more. It has a social aspect to it: people need to recognize that one has done well. Handling success modestly suggests behaving a certain way with others who do indeed recognize the achievement.

Again, humor's ability to fend off defeat in times of trouble is clearest when they are just that—temporary episodes. Morreall claims:

> When the person with a sense of humor laughs in the face of his own failure, he is showing that his perspective transcends the particular situation he's in, and that he does not have an egocentric, overly precious view of his own endeavors. This is not to say that he lacks self-esteem—quite the contrary. It is is because he feels good about himself at a fundamental level that this or that setback is not threatening to him. The person without self-esteem, on the other hand, who is unsure of his own worth, tends to invest his whole sense of himself in each of his projects. Whether he fails or succeeds, he is not likely to see things in an objective way; because his ego rides on each of the goals he sets for himself, any failure will constitute personal defeat and any success personal triumph. He simply cannot afford to laugh at himself, whatever happens. So having a sense of humor about oneself is psychologically healthy.[17]

Here the individual-based approach combined with the perspective of the basically thriving person leads to general claims which lack credibility. When a black South African attempts to escape from permanent poverty and fails time after time, a sense of humor is not going to make those failures less threatening. Failure means being trapped in permanent poverty, and this *is* threatening—to the conditions of the person's daily life, to personal fulfillment, and to self-esteem. The lack of self-esteem is not the problem but the result of it. The problem is the imposition of a devastating life situation on a person who is powerless to overcome it. A sense of humor may be retained, but if so and if it is in some way valuable, this is not because it can bring about the kinds of wonders Morreall refers to. Even more disturbing is Morreall's implied characterization of the contrasting type of person, the person who does *not* approach failure with a sense of humor. This person now lacks self-esteem, is not objective, has an ego problem, and is in fact psychologically unhealthy. These seem to be presented as serious personal defects. Such a general characterization may indeed apply to someone privileged who attaches too much importance to some temporary and fairly contained failure. Such events are not seriously threatening to someone with security, resources, and social status. But it is not a fair characterization of the millions of people living without recourse in a desperately miserable situation. It is little wonder that self-esteem is hard to sustain in such circumstances. Furthermore, many societies have structures which depend on some members lacking self-esteem and so being nonassertive. Given the societal mechanisms at work, some groups of people are virtually trained to lack self-esteem. In all these kinds of cases the failure is not the individual's, but the society's.

THE PERSPECTIVE OF THE SOCIALLY POWERLESS

I see no reason to believe that the perceptions of the socially powerless are any bit less "objective" than those whose life situation and self-esteem have been nurtured by the structure of their society. To imply that such people are psychologically unhealthy compounds the offense. Millions are living in conditions where the "failures" are failures to escape a permanently devastating life situation. If as time goes by they approach these failures with less and less humor, this is not inevitable, but it is still a perfectly rational response. There is no reason to suppose it signals psychological ill health. For such a person failure has nothing to do with overassessing personal qualities or skills or potential, and nothing to do with having "his ego [riding] on the goals he sets for himself."[18] For these millions, failure is an imposable condition. Morreall is in danger of a concept of psychological health that can be met only by those the society allows to thrive, and in danger of ascribing the stigma of mental ill health to the rest. In most societies, there is a general skepticism about the judgment of anyone deemed to be mentally ill, but here that means that the reports, pleas, and protests of those without power are all undermined. When we read, as one of Morreall's reasons for the desirability of humor, that it makes us "more accepting of things the way they are,"[19] we should be alerted to a serious problem in perspective.

A person's nonpeer status may differ according to the situation involved. A man may have little power as a manual laborer in a Mexican factory and yet have great power in the relationship with his spouse. A woman may have little power in the spousal relationship while having great power with respect to their young children during the ten hours a day they are alone at home with her. There are, though, in any society those who are nonpeers in so many different respects that they are generally powerful or generally vulnerable. For the vulnerable who are lacking in power of any significant kind, what is morally appropriate is not "bringing things down to size." On the contrary, there need to be successes which are then celebrated to the full. Egos should be much stronger. Self-assertiveness, not modesty, needs nurturing, and so on. In short, things need "boosting up to size," not bringing down to size.

Humor is valuable to those who are deprived of appropriate power, but not for the reasons cited by Morreall. The humorist George Mikes points out that "laughter is the only weapon the oppressed can use against the oppressor. It is an aggressive weapon and a safety-valve at one and the same time"; "the joke is an art of rebellion at its best."[20] In the First World War the British made fun of the "invincible" German military line in a song about "hanging up the washing on the Siegfried Line." In the years before and during the Second World War there were stand-up comics doing ludicrous impressions of prominent Nazis in just about every theater in the Allied countries. In America, Charlie Chaplin gave an unforgettable performance in the film *The Great Dictator*, perfectly mimicking every one of Hitler's grandiose gestures. Underground newspapers in occupied countries included anti-Nazi cartoons, and once in a while recent arrivals in concentration camps risked their lives by circulating some joke or other. When people are faced with oppressive power, sometimes on a massive scale, acts of humor may not reduce that power, but they do tend to boost the morale of the oppressed. Perhaps they may be encouraged to rebel in more effective ways if there are any, or at least they may be able to better defend themselves against a sense of being overwhelmed and defeated. But these reasons for valuing humor are very different from those cited by Morreall.

Accounts of the desirability (or otherwise) of humor *in general* may be inappropriately influenced by the security and power of the person's life situation. It is easy to overgeneralize from the kind of situation we find most familiar, yet as we have seen, humor may be desirable for very different reasons, depending on the life situation and the power relations involved. There may well be no one set of reasons which holds for all life situations.

Also the power relations at work affect the moral acceptability (or otherwise) of *particular instances* of humor. I will explore one form of this second connection by examining the notion of "put-down humor" and the related moral issues.

PUT-DOWN HUMOR

When humor occurs in social situations where nonpeers are involved and the subject of the joke is present, there are understandable trends. These trends set the stage for two expected results: the subject of the joke "taking it," and the "bystanders" joining in.

Put-down humor that is successful typically involves two factors: (1) the social situation, and (2) the content of the joke. A put-down joke that can be fairly safely counted on to succeed will involve the joke-teller having as much power as the bystanders and more power than the subject of the joke if the subject is present. Being as powerful as the bystanders brings with it the minimum security typically needed for initiating this kind of joke. The subject's being less powerful (if present) makes it likely that the put-down is successful in that the subject will "take it."

But this is not enough to make the joke a put-down. The joke-teller might use a more powerful situation to "boost up" the subject in some way. Or the joke might focus on a kind of delightful innocence that, say, a child exhibits by some misdirected or ineffective action. A put-down joke involves something about the joke's content (as well as the situation), but this feature is nothing so simple as the joke's involving a false claim. Not all jokes involving false claims are put-downs. Parents sometimes use their powerful position to raise the self-esteem of a child by telling very simple jokes involving transparently false claims. When young Susie is scared she will be too nervous to sing loud enough in her solo, her father gleefully declares that "Your mom and me, we know better than that. We made a point of getting a seat right on the back row, and we're taking thick woolly ear muffs along as well. We've told them, they're going to have to watch those windows when you let it rip." Parents have been boosting the self-esteem of their children for centuries this way.

More surprisingly, put-down jokes may involve no false claim. Consider the following, for example: "What is long and black? An unemployment line." The main claim of this joke was basically true, because the joke was circulating in a locality where racism had left a disproportionate percentage of black people unemployed.

In a case of put-down humor the content of the joke involves lowering the status of the subject in some way—or in delighting in the subject's already lower status.[21] This can be done in various ways. Some content is explicitly degrading in that it is aimed at lowering the physical, moral, or intellectual character of the subject. But there are more subtle ways.

Roughly speaking, a put-down joke is to do with the joke-teller's aggrandizement or relishing of power, or, in some cases, resentment of another's appropriate level of power. The *put-down content* can reflect this in three main ways: (1) it can attack the power status the subject of the joke has (including the abilities, moral character, or moral standing of the subject), either by attempting to present them as less or by trying actually to lessen them; (2) it can try to justify some inappropriately lesser power status of the subject; (3) it can delight in or celebrate the lesser power status of the subject. Let's see how these three ways function, considering first situations when the subject is present.

PUT-DOWN HUMOR WITH THE SUBJECT PRESENT

When the subject is present, a typical case of successful put-down humor between nonpeers will involve both the usual social situation of joke-telling between nonpeers (namely, the joke-teller is more powerful than the subject of the joke and the others are predictably going to join in), combined with put-down content. Here the joke-content targets the lesser power-status of the subject.

The three main ways in which this can be done (following options [1]–[3] above) all raise morally objectionable possibilities. Thus: (1) the joke can attack the already lesser power status, either by presenting it as less than it is or by trying to make it less; (2) if that lesser power status is socially constructed and morally objectionable (so the person should have more power), then the joke may attempt to make the difference in power seem innocent or even attractive, may seek to justify it in some way; (3) if the power difference is socially constructed but morally justifed—or is a genuinely natural occurrence—then the joke's content may amount to a celebration of the difference.

Celebration is a concept that is rarely mentioned in philosophical ethics and yet it has considerable moral significance. It may or may not involve elaborate rituals, but an act of celebration is a way of expressing and communicating delight in something. My celebrating something signals that I hold it to be basically a good thing and worth applauding. Typically celebrations involve more than one person: in one way or another others are invited to join in.

Now consider the significant difference between a child's intellectual abilities and those of an adult. Although the joke may involve no false claim, to make a joke about the difference in intellectual power where the content unfavorably highlights the lesser abilities of the child is to celebrate something we have no business celebrating. Even when the nonpeer status is unavoidable (as here), we have grounds for not welcoming it. A significant difference in power brings with it the danger of abusing the greater power with impunity, perhaps even without conscious awareness.

This danger is surely so familiar and so inherent in the situation that where there is a choice, unequal power relations should be entered into only with the soundest of moral justifications and with reluctance. We are rightly uneasy about anyone who delights in accepting power as such, since it signals a lack of the proper caution appropriate to having power over others. The same signal can be given via the content of some jokes.

When the social situation and the joke's content are so aligned that a standard incident of put-down humor occurs, the subject of the joke now becomes the victim of the joke. Not all subjects of jokes are victims. Joking between peers, even mutual teasing, may involve no genuine victim, and no serious prudential contraints prevent their "fighting back." But intimacy of affection is no guarantee of genuine peer status. In many families, for example, children and teens are, with good cause, prudentially constrained in their responses to put-down jokes from parents.

Put-down humor can thus be a way of reinforcing a difference in power between the joke-teller and the subject. Furthermore, when some group of more powerful people habitually direct put-down humor against a less powerful group, the nature of the offense becomes far removed from a private matter between two individuals. Focusing on sexist humor, Merrie Bergmann writes that "a sexist joke is not an isolated event in which a woman is harmlessly teased or ridiculed."[22] In such circumstances the use of put-down humor becomes a political weapon. The psychologist Naomi Weisstein notes, "humor as a weapon in the social arsenal constructed to maintain caste, class, race, and sex inequalities is a very common thing."[23] We can easily underestimate the moral significance of humor between nonpeers.

PUT-DOWN HUMOR WITH THE SUBJECT ABSENT

If we move now to situations where the subject of the joke is not present and the joke cannot be traced to the joke-teller, then some things change. The subject of the joke may well be more powerful than the joke-teller. Some of the war examples given earlier fit this description.

One of the three forms of put-down content is still possible in this situation, namely, form (1) above: the content can attack the power status the subject of the joke has, either by attempting to present it as less or by trying actually to lessen it. If the subject has greater power but of a morally objectionable kind, then jokes with put-down content become valuable weapons of the oppressed against the oppressor. The oppressed cannot be counted on to retain the psychological resources for this, but where they do, such put-down humor may be the only recourse to hand. It may not genuinely lessen the power gap, but it may for some time be a buttress against coming to see the power difference as appropriate or "natural" or simply overwhelming. For these reasons, not all put-down jokes are morally objectionable. Some reflect the best of the human spirit's resistance to being dominated.

If the more powerful subject has morally justifiable constructed power, then the situation is not as clear cut. Morally unacceptable put-down jokes can occur about a subject in a more powerful position who justly undertakes the responsibilities involved. A frequent target is anyone who belongs to a group historically denied power who then legitimately moves into a more powerful position. For example, vicious put-down humor has been directed toward judges who are members of ethnic minorities, priests who are women, and politicians who are homosexual. Even if not present at the time, the incidents tend to filter back to the subject even if the actual joke-tellers are unidentified, and a subject who hears of the jokes must overcome their potentially unsettling effects. When the sniping is selectively aimed in this way, sustained over time, and from a variety of people, the humor becomes a form of harrassment. The bare fact of the subject's having overall more power does not provide automatic moral permission for put-down humor.

INDUCING SELF-ATTACK

While reflecting on put-down humor, I wish to consider a revealing phenomenon which occurs typically where the subject of the joke is present (and understands the joke) and when the joke-teller is far more powerful than the subject and at least as powerful as the others present. In these circumstances the joke is usually successful. The bystanders become secondary agents and there is no significant retaliation from the subject. In fact it typically means that the subject too laughs at the joke and so becomes a secondary agent—as well as victim.

Even a writer as astute as Ronald de Sousa fails to appreciate this. In his book *The Rationality of Emotion*, he writes, "in the standard case a phthonic [malicious] joke requires a butt or victim, and the butt of the joke is someone who typically does not laugh."[24] But in the realm of nonpeers, this is not typical. The subjects are manipulated into joining in the laughter at themselves, even though this is morally inappropriate. Two factors are usually at work. In the first place the situation often arises without warning and is over quickly, and there is a strong social expectation that we laugh at the joke. Subjects may realize only sometime afterward just what role they were placed in and how objectionable the joke's content was. But even if the subjects acquire skills of exceptional alertness, the second factor, prudence, remains. Often it is unsafe to retaliate or not join in. Ultimately the prudential constraints are what induce the subjects to become self-demeaning. If subjects see the nature of the joke in time, they may decide not to laugh—but they may well pay a price. They are now "poor sports," "no fun," "too touchy to laugh at themselves," and so on (none of which is a fair comment in the circumstances). In short, they are revealing embarrassingly defective characters. In addition, the refusal to defer to the more powerful may be remembered by the joke-teller in other contexts. The victim who laughs is compliant. The one who does not is signalling "independence," often more than the manipulative joke-teller cares for. The silent victim is "a difficult person," "surly," and "insubordinate." All this is likely to be remembered in future decision-making.

Placing or inducing someone into this self-demeaning role via prudential constraints is a moral offense over and above the content of the joke. If there is something significantly wrong with the joke's content, then that is one thing. To deliver the content in such a way that the victims become secondary agents endorsing the content (by joining in the laughter) is a second thing. The illusion is that using a joke makes it all harmless, but really it is just a great deal safer for the joke-teller. Telling the content straight may not provoke a retaliation or rebuttal, but even if the prudential constraints tempt someone not to object, still, the victims are now just victims, pure and simple. Constrained silence is bad enough, but it is not on a par with their actively taking part in a morally objectionable attack on themselves or their situation. Such participation leaves reflective victims disapproving, even ashamed, of their part in the act. The victims have been induced to become self-violating and this is a corruption of the proper attitude they should have to themselves. It is a further assault on their integrity and self-respect over and above the sheer content of the joke. When it happens repeatedly and fairly systematically (like the denigrating "wife jokes" at weddings or engagement parties), the message to the targeted group is powerful.

Put-down humor, then, can be controlling. It can manipulate the more vulnerable subjects not simply into silence, but into more active compliance with jokes that demean them. When such morally inappropriate control is combined with put-down content, humor can become oppressive.

ACTS, ATTITUDES, AND OPPRESSIVE RELATIONSHIPS

Before leaving this examination of put-down humor, I wish to mention briefly an extension of the notion of the subject's being absent at the time of the joke, namely, cases where the subject is not literally absent, but is unable to grasp the joke's content. Jokes about young children, about people with certain kinds of serious illness, and about animals can fall in this group. In daily life the offense of the put-down joke has usually centered around "hurt feelings" on the part of the subject, with consequently little restriction on humor when the subject cannot or will not be "hurt." So I have often wondered what it is about these cases that still strikes me as morally wrong. Even if put-down humor in these instances does not lead to an increased tendency to morally dubious humor in other cases where the subject would be hurt, I would still argue that some things are amiss.

In the first place, there is the underlying moral objection to the aggrandizement or relishing of power, to the savoring of an attack on the less powerful. And there is an extra element of cowardice involved in these kinds of cases. The concern here does not depend on the effects of the action but has to do with a disturbing attitude toward unequal power. That attitude can be in evidence even though the joke's subject does not feel hurt by the joke.

Second, I believe that the relationships involved can be morally unsound even if no one's feelings are hurt. In fact, in this work I will argue that distorted relationships lie at the heart of civilized oppression. This is obviously a major claim, so I will begin some preliminary work on it in the next chapter and develop it throughout the work.

When mentioning these moral concerns about humor, a predictable objection is usually raised: that taking these concerns seriously would ruin the spontaneity of humor. Humor should be sparkling, quick witted, born of the moment, but if people begin to think about the content of jokes and the social situation before actually articulating some piece of humor, then it would become strained and ponderous and dull. This objection is no more sound than the claim that concern about fallacious reasoning would ruin a person's ability to argue and reason "on her feet." The grain of truth in both cases is that for an initial period when the relevant perceptual skills are being acquired, spontaneity may be hindered. After that it flourishes as much as before, but with the automatic screening out of at least basic kinds of morally dubious put-down humor or invalid arguments. It does not prevent someone's having a robust sense of humor that sparkles instantaneously. Morally alert humor need not be tediously self-conscious and timid, just better aimed.

This examination of humor as a social act already points to some of the crucial points that will be developed throughout this work. Briefly here, the first main point is that when things are morally amiss, there may be no flashing red lights, no twitching antenna, nothing but the familiar and apparently innocuous incidents of daily life. If we look across the room at a party and see a group of people all laughing at someone's joke, how could anything be wrong? They are all enjoying themselves, surely? There is nothing eye-catching to nudge us into more careful reflection here, and not surprisingly given the absence of violence, most civilized oppression shares this feature.

When Mikes, for example, speaks of laughter as a weapon for the oppressed, the oppressed are spoken of only in terms of politically oppressed "lands," the suggestion seeming to be that any land with a "democratic" government and not under foreign control is free from oppression. It seems even a professional humorist can lack perception about the social dimensions of humor.

The second main point is that nonpeer relationships often play a major role in these less visible moral wrongs. These relationships may well be morally justified and soundly maintained, but they are inherently hazardous. For example, there are a number of ways in which the socially privileged can safely take the initiative where other people cannot, humor being just one of the ways. But a general advantage like this brings with it the danger of abusing it with impunity, and without even being aware of how often the advantage is exercised.

Third, a great deal of such abuse involves no malicious intention, and contributing agents are often unaware of anything amiss. People who repeatedly use put-down humor against the already vulnerable may have no intention of unsettling the subject of the joke, let alone damaging the person's self-respect. This is especially likely where the humor involves long-standing social habits, as the "wife jokes" do.

Fourth and relatedly, the victims are typically constrained in various ways, including in their communications with the contributing agents. Many victims of inappropriate put-down humor are compliant, living with the sting and humiliation of the jokes rather than risk being scorned as someone with no sense of humor, or risk annoying a more powerful person with plenty of future opportunities to retaliate. Put-down humor in the kinds of cases mentioned often involves unwitting but still inappropriate control of the victims.

NOTES

1. Laurence M. Thomas, *Vessels of Evil: American Slavery and the Holocaust* (Philadelphia: Temple University Press, 1993).

2. Plato, *Republic*, III, 388e-389a, trans. F. M. Cornford (London: Oxford University Press, 1945), 78.

3. Sometimes assessing the desirability of humor may be affected by some general theory of laughter a person holds. The traditional contenders for such an account are the Superiority Theory, the Relief Theory, and the Incongruity Theory. Roughly, a Superiority Theorist (like Hobbes) claims that humor involves a

person's feeling superior in some way as a result of some favorable comparison. A Relief Theorist (like Freud) refers to some physiological function of laughter, typically, the releasing of excess energy. The most popular theory, the Incongruity Theory, claims that humorous laughter is directed at something incongruous, something which does not conform to our reasonable expectations; past associations are shattered. (Schopenhauer and usually Kant are classified as Incongruity Theorists.) The three theories are a jumbled mix, two being primarily functional accounts, and the other referring to the content of the piece of humor. They are not genuinely exclusive accounts, and I would argue that no one of the theories gives an adequate account of all humor. Sometimes the content is humorous, sometimes the situation makes otherwise mediocre content funny, sometimes a verbal skill makes it funny, regardless of the actual content, and so on. So rather than introduce my work on this, I will just mention in passing that someone holding the Superiority Theory (which I do not) could reasonably find humor morally dubious in some general way. Hobbes, for example, claims that laughter "is incident most to them, that are conscious of the fewest abilities in themselves; who are forced to keep themselves in their own favour, by observing the imperfections of other men." (*Leviathan*, ed. C. B. MacPherson [Harmondsworth, England: Penguin, 1968], Part I, chapter 6, 125.)

4. Oliver Goldsmith, "The Deserted Village," line 122, in *The Poetical Works of Goldsmith, Collins, and T. Warton*, ed. George Gilfillan (Edinburgh: James Nichol, 1854), 18.

5. Fourth Earl of Chesterfield, Letter: March 9th, 1748, in *Letters of Philip Dormer Stanhope, Earl of Chesterfield, with The Characters*, vol. I, ed. John Bradshaw (London: George Allen & Unwin, 1892), 94.

6. Chesterfield, Letter: October 19th, 1748, vol. I, 164.

7. Chesterfield, Letter: March 9th, 1748, vol. I, 94.

8. Frank Moore Colby, *Imaginary Obligations* (New York: Dodd, Mead, 1904), 286.

9. John Morreall, *Taking Laughter Seriously* (Albany, N.Y.: State University of New York Press, 1983), chapter 8, "Humor and Freedom," 106, and nearly all of chapter 10, "Humor and Life." I wish to acknowledge Morreall's invaluable work on the philosophy of humor. It is a rare achievement for someone to create a "respectable" field of study where none was recognized before, and it is largely thanks to the hard work and excellence of Morreall that we can now speak of "the philosophy of humor." Apart from his own work in the field, he has brought together a now standard anthology, *The Philosophy of Laughter and Humor* (Albany, N.Y.: State University of New York Press, 1987).

10. Morreall, *Taking Laughter Seriously*, 122.

11. Morreall, *Taking Laughter Seriously*, 128.

12. Henri Bergson, *Laughter: An Essay on the Meaning of the Comic*, trans. C. Brereton and F. Rothwell (London: Macmillan, 1911), 5.

13. Richard B. Sheridan, quoted in *The New Dictionary of Thoughts*, originally compiled by Tryon Edwards, rev. and enlarged by C. N. Catrevas, Jonathan Edwards, and Ralph Emerson Browns (Garden City, N.Y.: Standard Book Co., 1957), 732.

14. Oliver Goldsmith, *The Vicar of Wakefield*, ed. Ernest Rhys (London: Walter Scott Ltd., 1889), 43.

15. E.g., Pamela Bradney, "The Joking Relationship in Industry," *Human Relations* 10, no. 2 (May 1957): 179–87; Rose L. Coser, "Some Social Functions of Laughter," *Human Relations* 12, no. 2 (May 1959): 171–82; Rose L. Coser, "Laughter Among Colleagues," *Psychiatry* 23, no. 1 (February 1960): 81–89.

16. See Morreall, *Taking Laughter Seriously*.

17. Morreall, *Taking Laughter Seriously*, 106.

18. Morreall, *Taking Laughter Seriously*, 106.

19. Morreall, *Taking Laughter Seriously*, 128.

20. George Mikes, *Humour in Memoriam* (London: Routledge and Kegan Paul, 1970), 91, 92.

21. Fifty students (who did not know about my work on this topic) were asked if they ever found jokes morally objectionable, and if they did, to collect some examples over a period of a few months. Apart from a small number of jokes about some tragedy or other (e.g., jokes about the *Challenger* shuttle disaster), the rest of their examples overwhelmingly had the same pattern: they were put-down jokes aimed at already disadvantaged members of society. The following is a representative sample. "Why are aspirin white? You want them to work, don't you?"; "Why do women live longer than men? They aren't married to women." [Ed Sullivan in a rerun of his show]; "Why are women abused? Because they just don't listen."; "How do you confuse Helen Keller? Put door-knobs on the walls." Others were even more objectionable.

22. Merrie Bergmann, "How Many Feminists Does It Take to Make a Joke? Sexist Humor and What's Wrong with It," *Hypatia* 1, no. 1 (Spring 1986): 63–82, 76.

23. Naomi Weisstein, "Why We Aren't Laughing Any More," *Ms.* 2 (November 1973): 49–51 and 88–90, 51.

24. Ronald de Sousa, "When Is It Wrong to Laugh?" chapter 11 in *The Rationality of Emotion* (Cambridge, Mass.: MIT Press, 1987), 291.

Chapter 2

Inner Workings

The lack of visibility that surrounds civilized oppression has a number of sources, and I wish to explore these further in this chapter. I will also suggest that if we are to give an adequate account of civilized oppression, we need to focus on the role of the underlying relationships.

RELATIONSHIPS AND TANGIBLE HARMS

It is a natural assumption that oppression consists of systematically inflicting harm on people and that civilized oppression, therefore, consists of inflicting harms of a less brutal kind. Certainly one can expect oppression to harm people, but there are serious limitations if we offer this as an account of oppression, even if we extend the concept of harm beyond its usual constraints to include fairly temporary psychological hurts.

In daily conversation and in philosophical literature, harms are often conceived of as fairly tangible sorts of things. For example, a recent news item announced that "a masked man with a knife burst into the home of an elderly couple and demanded money. Since they had none in the house, the man searched a few obvious places and then ran out in frustration. The couple were not harmed." We all know what this means, but it is interesting that in this common usage, being terrorized does not qualify as "being harmed."

In Joel Feinberg's *Harm to Others*, the main sense of "harm" found there has this traditional emphasis where being harmed leaves you "worse off" in some ongoing way. Harm, Feinberg writes, is a "setback to one's interest," where an interest is something one "has a stake in."[1] Furthermore, "passing unpleasantnesses are neither in nor against one's interests. For that reason, they are not to be classified as harms."[2] Harms for Feinberg seem to be ongoing and fairly tangible sorts of items. He claims that "very few of us have interests in contented states of mind or in avoiding disap-

19

pointment as such,"[3] or again, "there is no interest in not being hurt as such, though certainly . . . the absence of pain is something on which we all place a considerable value."[4] In fairness, Feinberg's focus is on the limits of criminal law, whereas I am concerned with moral issues concerning oppression. Still, the emphasis in his account has a plausible ring to it, and there are parallels to be found in ordinary usage. But if we focus only or even mainly on harm in this sense, we miss a great deal of what is involved in oppressive situations. And even when such harm is indeed oppressive, we gain no clear view of why and how it is oppressive.

A similar emphasis on the more tangible is also reflected in current theories of justice where the predominant view in recent years has been that justice is to do with distribution, especially of tangible goods such as income and employment. Attempts to add into the distribution less tangible items like self-respect or rights or power are problem-ridden, as critiques like Iris Young's reveal.[5] I find the role of relationships in an account of social justice far more central than this distributive model suggests or allows for.

Oppression obviously involves social structures and institutions, and it calls for political action. But oppression also reaches down into the lives of individuals, and some of the moral issues raised at this level are not readily seen. We need some way of making the relevant components of oppression more visible, and focusing on harm does not do the job. Feinberg does mention a second concept of harm where harming someone means the same as wronging someone or treating the person unjustly.[6] This unusual concept of harm is more relevant for my topic than is his other, more familiar, concept of harm; but to bring to light the more elusive features of oppression, it will be more promising and fruitful to redirect attention from the infliction of harm to the underlying relationships.

Suppose the homes of the Smith and the Mandel families are both destroyed by fire. The Smith's house catches fire when an unpredictable earthquake ruptures a gas line. The Mandel's house is burned down by the local neo-Nazi group. Given the increased fire services in the area after the fire and the replacement of gas fuel, the Smith's rebuilt house cannot burn down again from the same cause. Also, it is known that the local neo-Nazi group never further harrasses a family in any way after burning down the home. At that point, they always turn to some new victim. In a sense the harm to interests is the same in both cases: both families have lost their home and possessions. If they both have the same financial resources, both face the same struggle to replace the home. Neither family has grounds for an ongoing fear of a recurrence, and let us suppose they are both spared long-term trauma. Still they must deal with the shock and the feelings of displacement caused by the loss, even though all the psychological hurts are stipulated to be temporary. Do these count as harms?

It is a reasonable extension of the more usual concept where harm is more tangible and ongoing. If they count as harms, then the Mandels may be more harmed than the Smiths. They have not only lost their home, but it came about via a moral wrong, an injustice, and that often arouses extra feelings of anger, indignation, or depression.

But there is more to their situation than these additional (temporary) psychological hurts or harms. Although the Mandels know they are free from future harrassment, they nonetheless now have full knowledge of the local group's intense hostility and know that, because they are Jews, they are refused admittance into a relationship of respect and equality with its members. They are aware that they are trapped in morally distorted relationships they can do nothing about, and these inappropriate relationships matter in their own right. We can extend the conception of harm to include pyschological hurts, even fairly temporary ones, but this still does not capture what is most basic to an oppressive situation, namely, the underlying relationships.

As with a morally wrong act, there being a morally inappropriate relationship does not ensure that those directly involved are culpable. It will depend on matters like motives, possible negligence, complicity, whether they are capable of moral responsibility, and so on, but distorted relationships can occur without the prime agent being culpable. Perhaps someone has been relentlessly indoctrinated from birth into false beliefs about others in the relationships and lacks the abilities needed to self-initiate a careful critique. Of course, there may be moral grounds for trying to amend the relationship anyway, although again, as with immoral acts, this may be overridden by some even more urgent obligation.

Also, although such relationships often bring with them straightforward kinds of harm to finances, employment options, security of possessions, or even personal health and safety, they need not result in such harms. Sarah never consults her sixteen-year-old daughter, Andrea, about her goals and preferences, but chooses "for her." However, she always chooses what Andrea would have chosen if asked, and Andrea's interests are well served. For example, Andrea does not suffer the harms of being pushed into particular studies or sports or employment not suited to her talents. Nor does Sarah make the choices in a manner that is fierce, loud, or threatening. They are quietly made and Andrea's spirits are not crushed. She remains a lively and outgoing young woman, and let us suppose that she is not distressed by the lack of consultation. Nonetheless I suggest that, given the age of the daughter, the continual nonconsultation constitutes a significant distortion of what the relationship should be. I think this is so even if Andrea is growing steadily in maturity and independence by picking up good life skills elsewhere.

There are very many more cases where, given the options actually available to the person, the option involving an inappropriate relationship may involve no increase in fairly tangible harm, and may even reduce it. In fact it may be the best option with respect to this kind of harm. This pattern of available options is often the result of oppressive social structures rather than random misfortune. Still, someone faced with this choice finds that entering into the relationship brings the best practical results. In an authoritarian boarding school a pupil may find that being totally submissive and passive toward the most influential teachers, even when unfairly accused, results in being spared all the unpleasant chores and receiving bonuses like loans of useful books and excellent letters of reference. So while a morally inappropriate relationship is likely to bring interest harm to the victim, it is not logically guaranteed.

It is worth pointing out that sincere attempts to provide a recourse for some interest harm often founder because they leave some relationship untouched. I recall a situation where a blind woman with a guide dog was rejected as a potential tenant by a live-in manager, with considerable abuse and the declaration that "no pets are allowed." Various agencies immediately pointed out to her that it was illegal to refuse accomodation because of a guide-dog and that it would therefore be a simple matter to force the manager to reverse his decision. Many were baffled when she did not pursue this course. Only a few seemed to understand the importance of her point when she explained that "you can force him to let me live there, but no matter how he behaves from now on, you cannot change his abusive conception of me—and my guide dog." The relationship was not tolerable for her as tenant and would need a significant change in the manager's attitude before it would be, something that could not be forced upon him.

THE DIVERSITY OF RELATIONSHIPS

Relationships differ a great deal with respect to potential development, the richness and diversity of interactions, how longlasting they are, and so on. Two friends living in the same town have the potential for a rich, well-developed, and long-lasting relationship, whereas a road-test examiner and a student-driver do not. The latter pair will be together once, for an hour or so, in very restricted circumstances. These differences matter when we ask what qualifies as an inappropriate relationship. Not everything that goes wrong in an otherwise acceptable relationship does qualify. It has to involve some significant distortion.

In a well-established friendship there may be times when one or the other has a bad day and makes exaggerated or unfair remarks that cause anger or pain. A good long-term relationship with a lot of interaction can absorb some small offenses once in a while with no more than a hiccup effect. The same holds true for many other relationships which are fairly rich and longer-term.

However, a relationship can be both temporary and very restricted. It is natural to think of relationships in personal or family or occupational terms, where the distinction between specific interactions and the standing relationship is obvious. But the distinction between what people do and the underlying relationships can hold even in cases where the duration of the relationship is short. In that case a momentary lapse may undermine the whole relationship. Not enough about the relationship remains as it should be for it to qualify as sound. If I am selling train tickets and stop serving a shy youngster in order to answer a long and confused inquiry from someone older who just walks over to the counter and starts speaking, then in the one or two minutes it takes to untangle the confusion, much has gone wrong in my relationship with the first client. This tends to be acknowledged where there is clear harm to her interests, if, say, she just misses the only train for hours. But even without this tangible harm, I have already impaired the little that is involved in this relationship of ticket-seller and client. Where little is involved in the nature of relationship, it is easy for nearly all of it to be wrong—or equally, to be right. What counts as significantly wrong and how easily such unsoundness is achieved depends on what the relationship is.

DISTORTION BY ACT

If we ignore the diversity of relationships, we may assume that nothing as fleeting as an offensive comment can constitute significant impairment. Consider, for example, what Joel Feinberg says about receiving a rude comment.

> These experiences can distress, offend, or irritate us, without harming our interests. They come to us, are suffered for a time, and then go, leaving us as whole and undamaged as we were before. . . . An affront or an insult normally causes a momentary sting; we wince, suffer a pang or two, then get on with our work, unharmed and whole.[7]

It is tempting for someone who is secure and socially privileged to generalize about the insignificance of an affront or insult. Consider, for example, someone who is well known, securely placed in a well respected, high-income profession, and spared the disadvantages and humiliations that come to members of ethnic minorities, women, the physically disfigured, and others. A passing insult cannot threaten the many and im-

portant tangible goods so securely in place, nor does it often seriously
threaten the basic self-esteem so well supported by the many public signs
of respect. But we should not generalize from this. The only problem
Feinberg acknowledges is the possibility of hurt feelings, the "momentary
sting." But an insult or affront can indeed result in interest harm if directed toward someone vulnerable at a critical moment, say, in the first
moments of a job interview. And it can in some circumstances understandably shake a person's basic and justified self-esteem, and not because of some individual, psychological quirk or oversensitivity on the
part of the victim. Threats or damage to justified self-esteem might be
conceived of as threats or damage to the person's proper relationship to
himself, but in any case, speaking more generally, whether or not an affront significantly impairs a relationship depends at least as much on the
nature of the relationship as it does on the severity of the insult. It can
occur, especially with a relationship that is very temporary and restricted
and where what is said is vital to the nature of it. The staff member at the
restaurant whose sole job is to welcome customers can significantly damage this relationship with one insulting comment; some potential customers may walk out because of it.

At this point we should distinguish two questions: whether a relationship is significantly distorted and whether a relationship is significant or
important to any of the people involved. In the restaurant example, the
relationship is much distorted, given the little that it involves, but the relationship may not be important in the life of the customer.

It would be a mistake, however, to assume that if a relationship *is* very
temporary and restricted, it is sure to be unimportant to the people involved unless accompanied by serious effects on tangible interests. Even
without such effects, some temporary relationships are very important in
other ways. A degree ceremony marks a major achievement in students'
lives, and consequently the university representative who expresses the
congratulations—in about four or five seconds—is in a relationship that
matters to many students. A whispered insult instead of the appropriate
congratulations would wreck what the relationship should be, namely, an
institutional representative drawing public attention to and celebrating
the student's achievement. Interestingly, given the relative status of the
two people here, the student has been *placed* in a wrong relationship and
will probably be staggering off the stage with the relationship unamended and in a sense, over.

Feinberg does make one exception to his general claim about the trivi-
ality of an affront. He does allow that harm can arise from experiences
of being insulted: "If the experience is severe, prolonged, or constantly
repeated, the mental suffering it causes may become obsessive and incapacitating, and therefore harmful."[8] In fact, the insults need not be so very

prolonged for harm to occur, nor need they, of course, be repeated by the same person. A temporary relationship may in fact become important if its distortion involves one of a number of similar acts which cumulatively result in some type of harm to their recipient. Suppose John is spending the week in a small town and the person serving him at the post office does so with hostile stares and blatant rudeness. John may feel bad for a moment or two and then shrug it off. But if John is black and finds the same bigotted reponse in quite a few places in the same town, in the grocery store, restaurant, garage, and library, then although all the temporary relationships may involve different people, still each contributes to some nonminor harm(s), like ruining his vacation. He returns home exhausted and humiliated.

But as with the Smith and Mandel case, I am suggesting there is more to this situation than the hurt feelings and distress, and the resulting spoiled vacation. Let's contrast this case with another. Suppose that against all the odds, five or six of John's friends all have disappointments, things going wrong, semi-emergencies of a practical kind, all in the same week, so that every one of them has a wretched time and behaves accordingly. Suppose that John, as usual, sees all of them throughout the week, whether in the parking lot, at the gym, across the backyard fence, or in the grocery store, and finds that one after another glares belligerantly where usually there is a cheerful greeting. They are unsympathetic, curt, and even ouright rude. These are distressing experiences, quite sufficient to ruin John's week and make it miserable. If he is spending his week of vacation time at home, his vacation could well be spoiled. But there is a difference between the two cases. In spite of all the distress he feels about how his friends have treated him that week, and even though he is taken aback by their behavior, the underlying relationships need not be unsound. It is sheer bad luck on John's part that his friends have all run into a bad patch at the same time. If John has known them all for many years and has overwhelming evidence of their general goodwill and affection, he may well conclude that whatever the explanation, it does not involve a collapse of the friendships.

In both situations John is distressed. He may even be more hurt by the rudeness of his friends, just because they are his friends. In both cases the accumulation of distress means that John's special week is ruined. But the relationships may be basically sound in the one case and morally inappropriate in the other. And this is a difference between the two cases over and above the psychological hurts or harms involved. Feinberg allows that offensive remarks may cause "mental suffering" that may become "obsessive" (a rather disturbing choice of term) and "incapacitating, and therefore harmful," but I am inviting us to look deeper and see that sometimes more is involved, namely, objectionable relationships.

I also claim that given the diversity of relationships, the experience need not be "prolonged or constantly repeated," or "severe" in any simple sense, for such a defective relationship to be involved. The insulted, graduating student is a case of that type. We should beware, then, of assuming that only dramatic events can significantly distort a relationship. Similarly, it is a mistake to assume that only long-lasting and rich relationships can be legitimately important to a person. However intuitively appealing, these assumptions are false.

I think we now have enough to support a basic claim about the role of acts in objectionable relationships. The relationship between the university representative and the student is impaired via the act of the insult, regardless of the representative's attitude. If, for example, the insult was made to win a bet and there was no malice or contempt felt, that would not save the relationship. The same is true with longer-lasting relationships. Sarah genuinely loves her daughter Andrea and wants only the best for her, but the acts of nonconsultation alone are, I suggest, sufficient to significantly impair the relationship. The point that emerges is that for many, if not all, relationships, certain acts (regardless of attitude) can render a relationship morally inappropriate, and in some circumstances a single act can. The whispered insult from the university representative is devastating to the relationship involved, whereas the long-standing, securely based friendships John has can remain basically sound in spite of the rudeness he experiences. (There would, of course, be single acts of some kinds that would render the friendships unsound.)

DISTORTION BY ATTITUDE

But just as it is possible to underestimate the role of acts in the soundness of some relationship, so too is it possible to overestimate it. In particular, although certain acts may be sufficient to impair a relationship, acting in the appropriate way may not be sufficient to establish a sound relationship. It is in the nature of many relationships that the appropriate acts alone are not enough to ensure a basically right relationship. A distortion can occur via mental state or mental act alone, via "attitude," as I shall say, as a useful umbrella term. All the normal physical acts involved in friendship have been performed by wartime spies who have not the slightest feeling of affection or caring toward the so-called friend, and who in fact may consistently have feelings of hostility. The acts alone do not make this relationship of friendship sound, since certain overall attitudes are crucial to the nature of a friendship. An attitude may be so inapproriate as to seriously distort a relationship or even disqualify any claim to the relationship (as here with the so-called friendship).

Of course, a person's acts do tend to reflect the person's attitudes, but they need not. Suppose Tim has been a celibate priest for a long time and is very happy with his vocation. It is important to him that people understand and accept his celibacy, since that is an important part of who he is. Kate finds him physically attractive, but this and the occasional involuntary passing thought or feeling that naturally occurs need not threaten their friendship. Kate, however, frequently indulges in extended daydreams, deliberately mulling over by the hour possible scenarios all ending with a sexual relationship between herself and Tim, all carefully concealed from him. Still, I suggest that these frequent and extended episodes seriously alter the relationship. I am not generalizing about sexually oriented daydreams, but what Kate is doing in these special circumstances is shaping a relationship that violates genuine friendship and lacks respect for the person he is. The stream of daydreams all involve Tim's violating one of his deepest commitments, and one does not have to share that commitment to believe that there is a form of betrayal involved here, a refusal to take seriously and respect that commitment.

Is there the possibility of distortion via attitude alone for all relationships? Could there be some relationships that are genuinely constituted by acts alone, where attitude is irrelevant? Presumably the most likely place to look is at relationships that are temporary and very restricted in scope, but even here the answer is not obvious. And certainly it is untrue for a number of important longer-term relationships where attitude is clearly a constitutive element.

But at this point there is again an important distinction to be drawn, between asking: (a) whether any relationship is constituted by acts alone; and (b) whether one person having dealings with another is ever free from the possibility of having an inappropriate attitude toward that other person. An affirmative answer to question (a) does not guarantee the same for (b). The reason is that there might be some very basic kind of relationship (or more than one) that should hold between all—or nearly all—humans (and possibly others), and if that relationship essentially involved an attitude as well as acts, then accompanying all—or nearly all—fairly specific relationships would be this basic relationship involving an appropriate attitude. Nearly always, then, there would be the possibility of having a significantly inappropriate attitude toward those one has dealings with. And if the generally required relationships had some special moral priority, then this would be at least one of the ways in which more specific and incompatible relationships would be screened out as unsalvageable in most if not all circumstances. If they are in conflict with the requirements of some most basic and far-reaching relationship, then this would be one reason for deeming them to be morally inappropriate.

THE ROLE OF ATTITUDES IN RELATIONSHIPS

My suggestion that a viable relationship can become morally distorted by someone's inappropriate inner attitude alone will be resisted by many, but not by everyone. In J. Kellenberger's recent book, *Relationship Morality*, he argues for the moral relevance of "interior action" when considering the soundness of some relationships.[9] He calls upon the earlier work of Herbert Morris who presented a series of situations where the person is less and less directly connected with an obviously immoral action, and yet where, even so, a case can be made for claiming some moral guilt. In the first case, one man murders another.[10] In the second, a man "with precisely the same state of mind" performs the same acts, but unknown to him, his victim has died of a heart attack seconds before being stabbed. As Morris notes, it is quite reasonable to claim that the second person is as morally guilty as the first.[11] In a third case, a man intends to kill, takes steps toward doing so, and then abandons the scheme because he is afraid of being caught. Says Morris, "there are no marks to be placed on the credit side of his moral ledger sheet. It may even be claimed that 'in the eyes of God' he is indistinguishable from the last step attempter."[12] These different cases are held together by the fact that the person forms the intention to kill and either does kill, or would kill if it could be safely done. This is why many are fairly sympathetic to the claim that if the agents are morally assessed, all of them would be guilty to some degree. All of them are apparently murderers or would-be murderers.

But where Morris is at his most challenging is in the last case in his series.

> The class of the guilty widens considerably when we consider a man's char-
> acter and what he desires to do. Suppose that a man desires to kill. Suppose
> he firmly believes that were he to possess Gyges' ring, with its capacity to
> make him invisible, he would kill. All that holds him back is fear. Is he any
> less guilty than the man who turns back at a later stage because of fear?[13]

It is not clear that Morris fully endorses the suggested position, but he does find it plausible. He describes this last set of people as those who have "accepted desires to do acts that are wrong," where by "accepting desires" Morris means they are "either persons who form intentions to realize their desires or, if having desires, they do not form such intentions, fail to do so for reasons that are not morally creditable."[14] Either way, it is the intention to do wrong that is central.

Morris is now well on his way to his claim that accepting a desire can damage a relationship, even if the corresponding action is not under-taken. But we should not be detoured by his particular emphasis on the culpablity of the agent. The main focus in my chapter here is on morally inappropriate relationships. I am claiming that a viable relationship can become morally inappropriate by attitude alone, but this need not involve a morally cupable agent.

In Morris's example a husband "forms the intention to commit adultery."[15] Morris then lists three situations: the husband commits adutlery and his wife learns of it; he intends to but in fact does not, but his wife learns of his intention; and, he intends to, does not, and his wife does not learn of his intention. It is Morris's contention that not only the first two, but the third situation also harms the relationship. "But suppose she doesn't learn of his intention. The relationship has still been damaged, for it is defined partly by each partner being prepared to exercise restraint out of love and respect for the other."[16]

When Kellenberger takes up this example of Morris's, he makes the point that a person can "accept a desire" without forming the relevant intention. Even if someone has no thought of actually doing the action, the desire could be accepted by "dwelling upon and savoring the desire in fantasy," and this in itself could be "harmful and hurtful" to a relationship, like that between a married couple.[17]

I am sympathetic to Morris and Kellenberger on these points, having reached much the same conclusions myself. But I build in one limitation (which may or may not be acceptable to them). Although a relationship can become morally objectionable via attitude alone, this does not mean that every unfair or inappropriate thought, feeling, desire, or unfulfilled intention significantly damages the relationship in a way that renders it morally unsound. In the first place, the thought or feeling or whatever it is has to be concerned with something foundational to the relationship. In a standardly monogomous marriage, sexual fidelity is foundational. Second, whatever the mental item is, it does indeed have to be on a scale that transforms the relationship. What counts as something that "transforms" a relationship into one that is morally inappropriate obviously involves moral judgement, but as already mentioned, in many longer-term relationships an occasional unfair thought or untoward desire need not threaten the moral status of the relationship. A morally sound relationship is not the same as a morally perfect relationship. If a single desire or unfulfilled intention can transform a long-term relationship in the relevant way, it will have to be some truly foundation-shaking desire or intention.

Suppose a married woman watches a tennis match at the local sports club, finds one of the players sexually attractive, and for the first time in years, daydreams about a sexual encounter with someone other than her husband. Does this morally distort her marriage relationship? There is a big difference between this and someone who continually views men around her as fantasized sexual partners, with a constant series of day-dreams, and far more time given to thinking sexually about these men than about her husband. Even if her husband knows nothing about it, this habit distorts the relationship. So too does Kate's continual and extensive daydreaming about a sexual relationship with her friend, Tim, the celibate priest.

The best of friends sometimes have passing thoughts about each other that are unkind or unfair. Typically they are not significant enough to transform the moral soundness of the friendship. A person can be a reliable, compassionate, trustworthy, and affectionate friend and still have the occasional, passing feeling or thought that is unfair or inappropriate in some way. If the thought were voiced, it might cause temporary hurt feelings, but no lasting distress. Longer-term relationships that are fairly intimate have the potential for this kind of resilience.

But suppose that the passing thought of one friend, Carlo, *would* cause deep and ongoing distress in the other friend, Bob, if he knew of it. In fact, Bob would be so distressed, he would withdraw from the friendship and the relationship would collapse. Would this not prove that Carlo's thought is anything but trivial? If we knew this is what would happen, would it not indicate that the relationship is distorted by the "interior act," to use Kellenberger's phrase? That is to say, if we allow that thoughts, desires, and other mental items can in themselves render a relationship unsound, would this not be a prime candidate for such an item? Not necessarily. Suppose the thought *is* voiced. Then this particular relationship of friendship will become morally inappropriate, with one person thoroughly hostile and permanently distrustful, refusing to speak to the other, no longer going to social occasions where the other person is expected, and so on. Indeed, the friendship will collapse altogether. But judgment is involved in locating what accounts for this. If I am right about what good friendships involve, then a key question is whether Bob is being unreasonable in ending the relationship rather than simply being annoyed for a few days. Surely there can be some single, unfair comment where such temporary annoyance is all that is justified. Much depends on the nature and gravity of the remark, but the mere fact that Carlo makes the remark and Bob responds by ending the friendship does not mean it is a fair description to say that Carlo's remark rendered the relationship morally unsound (and in fact, brought about its collapse). In some situations the description should rather be that Bob's lack of all sense of proportion about an unfair but quite atypical remark from a friend rendered the relationship morally unsound (and, in fact, brought about its collapse). Whether or not Bob is culpable for having so little sense of proportion is a separate matter.

The best candidates for attitudes which in themselves make an otherwise acceptable relationship unsound are either single mental items of exceptional gravity (single desires, unfulfilled intentions, and so on), or an ongoing series of items (in which case, individually they may not be of the same magnitude). In longer-term relationships anyway, very few people can in practice consistently act in a manner at odds with an attitude they really hold. Sooner or later we can expect the attitude to show in the person's acts. But for the moment we are considering the most theoretically interesting combination where ex hypothesi there are all the appropriate acts but an inappropriate attitude. It is not unusual to hear the objection that in such a case, "all the goods of the relationship are delivered," so to speak. But this is not as plausible an objection as first appears.

DELIVERING ALL THE GOODS

Certainly nothing is established by the simple lack of awareness of the inappropriate attitude. Some relationships by their very nature involve certain attitudes as indispensible components, as does friendship. Even some very temporary relationships do. When a university representative has the role of handing out degrees at a graduation ceremony, a genuine appreciation of the students' work and achievements is central to that role. I am claiming that where a relationship is of this type, then if only the acts are appropriate, not only are all the "goods" not delivered, but what is delivered is not the genuine article.

The trouble lies with the claim that "all the acts are appropriate." When we say the acts are appropriate but the attitude is not, we mean that anyone looking on would see and hear nothing amiss in the person's overt behavior. All the right words are said in the right tone of voice with the right facial expressions. In fact, all the right physical moves, big and small, are there. But although the behavior may be just what we would expect, many of "the acts" in fact are not what they appear to be. They are illusory or deceptive, and if we are to describe them accurately, the available language will be very restricted. Where we would ordinarily say that "Mary spotted her friend and rushed over to give her a delighted hug" or "Kurt commiserated with his friend when he heard about the accident," these descriptions will need radical revision if there *is* no genuine delight or sympathy.

Where a relationship does involve a basic kind of attitude, as friendship does, many descriptions of acts naturally and reasonably include references to the feelings or desires that would be appropriate in the circumstances. Friends are typically pleased to meet one another, and normally, at least, one should be able to count on a friend feeling sympathy in the event of an accident. If, in fact, Mary and Kurt feel no such feelings for their "friends," if, for example, they fairly consistently feel hostility and contempt for them, then the usual and natural descriptions are simply false. It may be true that Kurt listens to the account of the accident, sighs and shakes his head in all the right places, and says how shocking and unnerving an accident like that can be—but ex hypothesi he does not commiserate and he does not listen sympathetically. These are not accurate descriptions of his acts. And many of our ordinary descriptions carry such implications about feelings, desires, or intentions, about "attitudes," as we have used this umbrella term. If we removed the words and phrases carrying such implications, then a great deal of ordinary language would be eliminated and we would be reduced to descriptions of behavior of a fairly robotlike kind. They could refer to physical actions, facial expressions, words spoken, and so on, but we would be deprived of the normal ways of speaking about the interactions between two genuine friends. The available descriptions, in fact, would be quite bizarre.

We are left with two options. Either we use the ordinary, attitude-implying language needed to refer to normal interactions between friends, spouses, colleagues, and so on, in which case the actions of neither Mary nor Kurt are in fact "appropriate." Or we move to the drastically reduced descriptions that refer to physical behavior alone with no reference to attitudes, in which case that behavior might indeed be appropriate. But that is insufficient to establish that the relevant acts are appropriate, and indeed, ex hypothesi they are not. Not only do the relationships of friendship and marriage in themselves involve some fundamental attitudes, but the descriptions of the individual acts to be expected within those relationships also involve reference to attitudes (in the wider sense). The usual acts of friendshp and the usual acts of love between spouses do not consist of behavior alone. That an onlooker might be misled about what seem to be someone's acts of friendship does not alter this.

In these theoretically interesting cases, like the relationships of Mary and Kurt, there is the most profound lack of authenticity in the overt relationship. What is "delivered" in the apparently overt acts is precious little when we describe them accurately. It is only when we cheat on the descriptions that we are tempted to say that "all the goods of the relationships are delivered." In cases like Mary's and Kurt's, a person may be in what I call "a covert relationship" not detectable via the behavior. Depending on the nature of the actual attitudes, the relationship can be morally inappropriate and can be so by attitude alone.

In fact, I will make a further claim: that attitude alone can involve justice issues. I can do someone an injustice, not just via acts, but via judgment, and not just via a pronounced judgment. My thoughts of someone can fail to do her justice, and if these thoughts are persistent and long term, there may be an ongoing attitude toward her which constitutes a morally objectionable covert relationship. It may or may not ever result in more tangible harm, depending on whether I am ever in a relevantly influential position. And it may or may not be possible in practice for the victim to know about the true nature of the relationship (or about any resulting more tangible harm). I see no reason why it should not be described as a matter of injustice, a matter of basic unfairness, even if the attitude happens not to result in some unjust overt act, nor even in some pronounced unjust judgment, but on this issue, I will just nail my flag to the mast and move on.

It is, however, worth saying that many people do care about attitude per se if we ask the right question. The question is not whether we would be disturbed by an objectionable attitude if all the acts were physically as expected and the thought of an inappropriate attitude had never crossed our mind. The answer to that would obviously be "no," since we would be epistemologically blocked from reflecting on the matter. The relevant theoretical question is something like this: suppose someone we have reason to believe (perhaps she has E.S.P. or receives divine communications or whatever) informs us that one of our long-term friendships is not what we think. In fact, we are told, although the physical behavior is just as expected, the attitude of the other person is unchangeably and fundamentally at odds with that behavior. The person lacks all affection and sympathetic interest and actually holds us in contempt. What would the response be? I think we would want to know which relationship, not out of curiosity, but because most of us would try to leave that relationship. We would not be reassured by the idea that the attitude would never obtrude into any piece of overt behavior. If anything, this would make it all the more sinister precisely because the covert nature of the relationship means we are quite defenseless against it. It is bad enough to lose a "friend," but it is far worse to believe you have a friend when you certainly do not.

We cannot safely substitute talk about harm for talk about relationships. Morally unsound relationships will probably result in tangible harms of various kinds, but they need not. They need not even result in hurt feelings. In fact in some of the most serious cases they do not, perhaps because the distortion arises via attitude alone, or because the victim has been trained to accept the relationship as appropriate. The mere fact that the parties in the relationship are psychologically content does not establish its moral soundness.

Unsound relationships that have no obvious interest harm attached are not easy to spot, not even when the distorted relationship is manifested in overt, but not obviously harmful, acts (like the case of Andrea and her mother, Sarah). And of course where the relationship is distorted via attitude alone, then it is invisible to bystanders and victims. But there

is yet another reason why the full significance of many morally objectionable relationships is hard to see, and that is because of the role of
accumulation.

CUMULATIVE DISTORTION

Such relationships can be cumulative in two senses. In the first place a
single relationship can be molded by a series of apparently trivial acts,
which cumulatively distort the relationship in an anything but trivial
fashion. Nothing visibly dramatic is involved, and one has to appreciate
the pattern of the acts before the nature of the problem is clear. Bystanders and even victims themselves often realize the problem very late in the
day in such circumstances. Realization is even harder to come by when
many of the contributory acts are acts of omission—something we will
find is not uncommon in oppressive relationships.

In the second place an individual can be involved in an accumulation
of distorted relationships so that many areas of life are affected. A person's life situation is located within a web of relationships, some temporary, some long-term, some more intimate than others, some involving
institutions. Everyone at some time or other is the victim of an objectionable relationship, whether trivial or major, but as the number and variety
of such relationships increase, a person's social standing and life situation
suffer a cumulative deterioration, at least, in the standard cases where the
distortions are revealed in acts. It is not a random matter who these victims are.

When we think of a socially privileged person, we think of someone
with a comfortable level of material provision. But in addition the person
is typically either on an equal footing with those around or has more social status and power than they do. This in turn brings with it the power
to initiate relationships, establish what their nature is to be, and even
more importantly, the power to object to a significantly inappropriate relationship and call for its amendment.

The accumulation of unsound relationships tends to occur especially
where there is no safe recourse, where the recipient is at risk even in indi-
cating that there is something wrong at all, let alone in objecting to the
nature of the relationship and calling for a significant change. For the
most vulnerable in society, therefore, they often continue unamended
and there is a cumulative deterioration of their relationship network over
time.

This chapter has focused on a number of points about relationships in
general, points that will be called upon in our examination of oppressive
relationships. We have described some of the shapes and sizes relation-

ships can have. Given this variety, we have considered the impact of acts alone and of attitudes alone on the quality of a relationship, and the varying levels of importance that acts and attitudes can have. We have looked beyond questions of harm to the cumulative deterioration of a relationship or a relationship network. We have noted that people can be trapped into having to choose between avoiding material harms and avoiding a morally objectionable relationship. In fact the avoidance of material harms may be both the reward and the mask of submission to an oppressive relationship. All of these matters point to the kinds of invisibilities involved in civilized oppression, and the inherent challenges in establishing the soundness of relationships will take on further significance as we go on to try and make visible what is involved in relationships of unequal power.

NOTES

1. Joel Feinberg, *Harm to Others* (New York: Oxford University Press, 1984), 33.
2. Feinberg, 45–46.
3. Feinberg, 43.
4. Feinberg, 47.
5. Iris Marion Young, *Justice and the Politics of Difference* (Princeton, N.J.: Princeton University Press, 1990), 15–33.
6. Feinberg, 34.
7. Feinberg, 45–46.
8. Feinberg, 46.
9. J. Kellenberger, *Relationship Morality* (University Park, Penn.: Pennsylvania State University Press, 1995), 73–77.
10. Herbert Morris, *On Guilt and Innocence* (Berkeley, Calif.: University of California Press, 1976), 117.
11. Morris, 117–18.
12. Morris, 122.
13. Morris, 122.
14. Morris, 124.
15. Morris, 124–25.
16. Morris, 125.
17. Kellenberger, 74–75.

Chapter 3

Having the Upper Hand

Oppression is rooted in distorted and morally inappropriate relationships, which underlie and contribute to harms of a more tangible kind (like poverty or unemployment). These relationships form the first level of inquiry, and they are typically relationships of unequal power. When these relationships are distorted in certain kinds of ways, oppressive relationships occur, and the existence of different degrees of social status and privilege in society provides fertile ground for such distortions. In fact I will argue that given all that social privilege involves, the danger of contributing to oppression is built in and can be prevented only by reflective and active measures. This in turn will point to certain challenging moral obligations which accompany privileged positions.

PRIVILEGE: BENEFITS AND POWER

Oppression involves a systematic and inappropriate control of people by those with more power. The oppressed are treated with disrespect, moral rights are denied or blocked, their lives are deprived of proper fulfillment, and they experience series of frustrations and humiliations beyond all normal bounds. Except for explicit denials of rights, none of these need be intentional, and when no physical force is used, a lack of awareness on the part of contributing agents is more common than not.

Oppression can involve death, unemployment, tedious employment, homelessness, or humiliation, but it is the contributory relationships that reveal the oppression. After all, we can be homeless because of a hurricane. Leaving someone homeless may well be oppressive, since a lot of oppression involves selective abandonment, but the sheer being without a home may not be.

Even something not attributable to natural causes, like a violent assault, may not be oppressive. Judith Andre writes that "oppression is systematic; a single assault—even murder—is not oppressive, for there are many categories of human evil besides that of oppression. The constant fear of attack, however, may well be oppressive."[1] Oppressive harms do not result from isolated acts of individual malice or negligence. One person cannot be repeatedly murdered, but murder can be used repeatedly to terrorize a group, and groups of people are the standard targets of oppression. This said, individual victims of oppression are typically recipients of cumulative harms, with a compounding significance not grasped by the more fortunate, especially when the oppression takes a civilized form.

For the word "privilege," standard dictionaries give phrases like: "a special advantage or benefit beyond the common advantages of others"; "a prerogative, advantage, or opportunity enjoyed by anyone in a favored position." We think of people with wealth, challenging careers, fine homes—people with more than the average share of assets that are socially constructed rather than natural.

Natural assets include the advantages of sight and hearing, of physical health and stamina, of being able to walk and run (all useful in certain kinds of physical emergencies, for example), but even these have a massive layer of socially constructed advantage added on to them in Western societies. Sighted, hearing, and ambulatory people are routinely favored in situations where difficulties for those lacking these features are irrelevant or could be constructively handled. Also, some other natural features are assets only in a socially constructed sense. Some height, weight, and appearance matters have no clear natural benefits, but are much favored socially. These features include far more than physical characteristics of the dominant racial group. Many other assets are more clearly socially constructed altogether, from the the vast salaries that some people receive, to the physical dominance of a church pulpit or the traditional "high table" in some university dining halls. The ongoing, major assets in this category—like the huge salaries—may be noticed, but many others are not if they are temporary and apparently insignificant. But such assets often function cumulatively, giving some individuals a series of advantages that benefit them in many incidents or interactions. It is not a random matter whose daily pathways are smoothed by such accumulations of small, socially constructed assets.

But there is an even greater danger in saying that a privileged person has more than the average share of socially constructed assets. The model of individuals accumulating benefits makes it easy to overlook a crucial type of benefit, which I will call "relationship power." Society is not composed of individual, isolated lives and life situations, but of a vast network of relationships, some consolidated into institutions big and small, some on a more intimate level, and the advantages of the socially privileged include power over other people in various relationships.

The same lack of attention to relationship power is found in most contemporary theories of justice where the central issue is the just distribution of the goods under social control.[2] The oversights become acute when the concept of justice itself is construed in terms of a just distribution of benefits within society. Critiques like Iris Young's in *Justice and the Politics of Difference* show that relationships and issues concerning them are not well handled on this model.[3] Although I focus more on how oppression reaches down into the lives of individual victims, Young and I and a number of others agree that "oppression and domination . . . should be the primary terms for conceptualizing injustice."[4] And civilized oppression has primarily to do with power-laden but distorted relationships.[5]

Although social privilege involves power, including temporary or ongoing relationship power, it is not any kind of power. The armed bank robber has power over the hostage, the son has power over his elderly and confused parent kept in the basement as a source of pension checks, but we would not refer to these relationship powers as forms of privilege. There is a justified condemnation of these exercises of power. Social privilege involves power that is generally accepted within the society, not generally condemned.

Judith Andre writes about a type of power traditionally attributed to women, namely manipulative power, and points out that "the mere belief that women are more manipulative than men is harmful to women," because it is a practice which is not only "socially forbidden," but also "morally defective."[6] Manipulation, after all, "is a form of deception,"[7] and "it is damaging to find oneself constantly forced to resort to actions which are *prima facie* wrong," both psychologically and morally damaging.[8] Andre concludes that "situations . . . in which an objectionable source of power is available to all, but utilized only by some, are likely to be oppressive."[9] Andre, then, would surely agree that privilege involves not just power, but power with the right kind of social status.

None of this means that privileged relationship power is bound to be morally unsound, but it does mean that pre-critically we will not see anything wrong with it, even when there is.

(INDIRECT) CONSEQUENTIAL POWER

Privileged members of society may have socially accepted relationship power with respect to their children, spouse, coworkers, and many people, including strangers, briefly encountered in day-to-day living. Also the relationship power may show itself in relationships of roughly equal power and influence where, for most people, the relationship would involve lesser power. Usually a loan applicant has less power than the bank manager in that specific relationship. Technically the power remains even if the applicant is highly privileged, since the manager decides about the loan. This is the "assigned relationship power" of the manager, and it is a form of "direct power" the one person has over the other.

It is tempting to think that all relationship power is direct or as some theorists describe it, "dyadic," and most of us tacitly begin with this assumption. As Thomas Wartenberg writes in his book *The Forms of Power*:

> According to this assumption, power is "located" within a dyad consisting of a dominant agent and a subordinate agent over whom he wields power. The salient feature of this conception of power is that it localizes power to a sphere of existence made up of the two social agents who constitute the central actors in the power relation itself.[10]

So if one person has power over another, an adequate account of that power need refer only to those two people. But relationship power is often not this direct. For example, the bank manager may be under pressure to decide favorably, even if the privileged applicant is unreliable and the privileges do not include wealth. Suppose that the applicant is a member of some European aristocracy, far from wealthy, but well known, influential, accustomed to being assertive, and with many social contacts— not a rare combination in some countries. Offended by a rejection, the applicant may complain to the manager and then, with the social clout available, to the regional manager, and to friends and contacts with financial assets to withdraw. So the applicant has unusual relationship power here in spite of being a poor candidate for a loan.

When relationship power is acknowledged at all, it is often oversimplified. If we see two or however many people in the relationship, then we think of relationship power as the direct power one of them has over the other, especially any direct power assigned via their social roles. The bank manager technically has the power to decide about the loan, but in the example there is more involved. The applicant has unusual power via the roles and actions of several third parties—wealthy friends and acquaintances, and the regional manager. I describe such power as "indirect," and indirect power can be potent indeed.

Wartenberg explains one form that indirect power can take. In his example of the student–teacher relationship, he looks at the teacher's power that comes from grading the student's work. The reason a low grade has an adverse effect on the well-being of the student, says Wartenberg, is because of "the way in which social agents peripheral to the student-teacher relationship react to it,"[11] for example, the medical school that rejects the student's application because of a failed organic chemistry course. He goes on to say that "if a student can be sure of never encountering an individual who will use a low grade as a basis for her treatment of the student, the fact of grading will not result in the teacher's having power over the student."[12] This perhaps goes too far, since grading involves some direct power because of the resulting embarrassment, disappointment, or the feeling of achievement, which can be strong responses if the grade is communicated in certain ways. (And direct power is exercised within the relationship in ways not having to do with grading.) But his main point is clearly correct—that considerable power comes from the expected consequential responses to the grade by influential other people, or as Wartenberg captures it, "the 'cooperation' of social 'others' with the 'intent' of the teacher's grading. . . ."[13] I call this form of power "(indirect) consequential power."

Wartenberg shows how this kind of power can function oppressively and invisibly by looking at the relationship between a husband and a wife in societies where "women have less access to many things which are normally deemed important for living a fulfilled life" and where "there is a whole series of economic facts that mean that women have a much harder time gaining access to social goods than do men."[14] As he points out, "her economic situation will be very different depending upon whether she is married."[15] So there are grounds for entering into marriage and staying married even if the relationship is seriously flawed. Thus "the power that husbands have is not the result of their own particular intentions"[16] and this explains why "the husband sees himself as not dominating his wife."[17] The unseen (indirect) consequential power bolsters his power to an inappropriate level and allows him to shape the marriage in ways which would otherwise cause his wife to leave. So she is under pressure not to exercise the right to leave a morally unacceptable relationship—which means she is oppressively controlled, whether the husband is aware of this or not.

Wartenberg's analysis is very insightful, but to come closer to understanding civilized oppression, we need also to articulate other forms of relationship power which often play unseen roles.

(INDIRECT) SUPPORT POWER

The bank manager has the assigned direct power to decide about the loan. The (indirect) consequential power of the manager lies in the way the applicant will be treated by others who "cooperate with the 'intent' of" the manager's decision. Let's say some potential business partners now will not set up a business with the applicant. But the applicant has a different type of indirect power if complaints and the imminent loss of some wealthy clients lead to pressure on the original manager to "review the decision." Consequential power arises once some direct and usually assigned power has been exercised successfully, and it is easy to assume that assigned direct power cannot be anything but successful. But this is false. Functioning at a stage prior to that of consequential power is another kind of power which I will call "(indirect) support power." It is harder to see because it often functions quietly to support the direct power in the relationship: the manager turns down the loan applicant— which decision stands—and so others now respond to the applicant in expected ways. But the decision stands only if the manager has indirect support power, especially from those in supervisory roles like the regional manager. In my example the applicant is able to undermine that support power.

Wartenberg writes as though being a teacher is enough to ensure reliable consequential power, but this ignores the role of support power. For most bank managers the support mechanisms will never undermine their assigned power. For this very reason they are likely to be oblivious to their importance. But when members of groups traditionally excluded from such positions begin to move into them, unreliable support power is not uncommon. The black police officer, the woman priest or professor, the openly homosexual politician, all have assigned powers because of their roles, but the first to move into such roles in some places may not be able to count on the support power that is taken for granted by their long-accepted colleagues, the white, male, physically able, heterosexual police officers, priests, professors, and politicians.

When this phenomenon occurs, those concerned are doubted more often, ridiculed more often, supervised more closely, maneuvered into the least critical decisionmaking whenever possible, and when challenged in some outrageous rather than legitimate way by someone over whom they technically have direct power, find no minimal and fair-minded support from peers who belong to the long-accepted groups, nor from those in supervisory roles. Fair-minded support here would involve an open-minded inquiry with no predisposition to suppose these members of traditionally excluded groups to have used power incompetently or immorally. If indeed the challenge or complaint turned out to be prompted by malice or prejudice, fair-minded support would also involve a sturdy indignation aimed at the culprit, not a dismissive shrug of the shoulders aimed at the victim.

A lack of support when exercising assigned direct power is not the only way in which a lack of appropriate support power is revealed. It can be uncovered when members of groups newly moved into positions of responsibility raise some concern, and it shows in the following ways: they find extreme skepticism about the concern, a predisposition to "explain it all away" without investigation, and not rarely their overall credibility is attacked or the matter is automatically construed as some purely individual, emotional confusion, particularly if it concerns ongoing oppressive acts. A past record of accuracy, reliability, and fair-mindedness on other issues may suddenly count for nothing once any such matter is addressed. In short, the reception of their concern is radically different from that accorded to those technically under their direct, assigned power.

In these various ways the support power is revealed to be very restricted and extremely shaky. Yet basically reliable support power is crucial if someone is to function without ongoing harassment and threats to important intangibles like personal or professional reputation. The gradual discovery that they are denied a reasonable level of support power is one reason why members of an oppressed group who have begun to move into positions of apparent power have nonetheless sometimes found themselves oppressed in those positions.

Support power can also be excessively high. Sometimes a privileged person has so much support power that even if some assigned power is clearly used incompetently or immorally, the person will not be brought to account. When this is generally known, the victims of the misused power know they have no genuine recourse, and this suppresses protest. In these circumstances people are being oppressively controlled, even when wronged—in fact, especially when wronged.

INTERACTIVE POWER

One final type of power I will call "interactive power." Roughly, it is the power to take the initiative in a relationship: in beginning or ending a relationship, in insisting on its being modified, and in taking a number of communication initiatives like the power to begin or end a specific contact (like a conversation), to insist on being listened to and on being given answers to reasonable and pertinent questions.

This form of relationship power is a major part of the assigned direct power in positions of responsibility. The bank manager has the assigned power to ask questions about the applicant's finances. The professor has the power to talk with individual students about their work. The employer may object to the secretary's regularly arriving late. This much interactive power we are usually aware of. We may even tacitly think of "accepted interactive power" as simply "the interactive power that is assigned in roles that are socially accepted." But this would be a mistake, and given the role of interactive power in civilized oppression, a far-reaching mistake.

To begin with, exercising these interactive powers month after month can result in a general disposition to be interactively dominant in contexts not covered by assigned power. Anyone who has attended social occasions like an office party or some parish party involving clergy and lay people, will see the same habitual patterns of interactive power there too. Even casual encounters in hallways and parking lots may display the same patterns. The general disposition also extends to many relationships having nothing at all to do with the position of responsibility, relationships where the other person has nothing to do with the social role and its assigned power. These cases include many of the brief exchanges with strangers that arise in daily living.

More than personal habit is involved. There is a social aspect to it in that this extension of interactive power is encouraged in members of the dominant social group, especially those who have roles with traditional prestige value. As already noted, in Western societies this still means able-bodied, white men, from a middle-class background, and not openly homosexual, who are in roles such as that of lawyer, doctor, priest, or business executive. The discrepancy in interactive power between the socially privileged and others is not readily grasped when the extension of power is unconscious. Neither is the full scope of the power fully appreciated.

I do not wish to oversimplify, since within the group of office staff, students, and laypeople some are even more subject to inappropriate use of interactive power than others, especially members of any groups still rarely found in the more powerful roles. More attention is paid to groups expected to produce the next set of "leaders," who at earlier stages need "grooming" or "cultivating." And these long-standing societal expectations change slowly.

For victims of inappropriate interactive power, conversations of importance are broken off or not listened to, explanations are interrupted, valuable contributions are not registered, protests are walked away from or not responded to, pertinent information is not received, and the person is not accurately known by those who blithely claim to know—something very damaging in this age of personal contacts and recommendations. It is remarkably easy for what look like minor differences in interactive power combined with an unintended selectivity in attention to block what should be basic knowledge of the victim and his/her forms of excellence, and to block appropriate interactions, including some important forms of communcation. In crucial ways the more vulnerable are easily silenced and immobilized.

These processes point to an important aspect of many day-to-day oppressive relationships, something that deserves a descriptive label of its own. The phenomenon I have in mind is the distortion of what I call "the public self." I will argue that a distorted public self is not simply a matter of an error of judgment, but rather a form of control with systematically protected errors.

THE PUBLIC SELF

Most of us begin with a simple view of how people get to know each other. It is just a matter of meeting, communicating, listening, observing, interacting, and generally paying attention. So when people find that no reasonable amount of interaction and communication results in their being known as well as they should be, they are often baffled. Even more unsettling than the lack of basic knowledge is the phenomenon of grossly inaccurate claims or beliefs about easily observable matters. Probably everyone has been in relationships where one of these two things has occurred, but it should be said immediately that those who are subject to them in a prolonged and systematic fashion are not randomly distributed throughout society. In particular, the phenomena are closely tied to being oppressed.

In *The Politics of Reality* Marilyn Frye notes that:

> A critical central range of the traits and abilities that go into a creature's being a person are traits and abilities that can be manifest only in circumstances of interpersonal interaction wherein another person maintains a certain level of communicativeness and cooperativeness. One cannot, for instance, manifest certain kinds of intelligence in interactions with persons who have a prior conviction of one's stupidity; one's clever pun is heard as a clumsy misuse of a word or as a *non sequitor* [sic]. . . . He can avoid seeing the critical central range of a woman's abilities and concerns simply by being uncooperative and uncommunicative and can, at the same time, be so without knowing he has been. The ease with which one can be uncooperative and uncommunicative while believing oneself to be the opposite is apparent from the most casual acquaintance with common interpersonal problems.[18]

Although Frye is speaking about sexism in particular, the same points apply to men and women in other kinds of oppressive situations involving poverty, unemployment, or racism. In interactions like these there is already a conception of the person functioning in ways that block perception of the person's actual attributes. These conceptions are notoriously difficult to dislodge, and they vary a great deal with respect to how explicit they are, how clearly acknowledged they are, and how surrounded they are by hostile emotions—and quite often no such emotions are involved. We are, for example, becoming increasingly aware of the role of negative stereotypes, images that vary from the brutally explicit to the disturbingly subtle.

I am concerned here with conceptions and images that take some public form, that is, they are revealed in some act or some feature of an act. They may be revealed in some claim, joke, physical gesture, facial expression, or tone of voice. The relevant contrast to "public" here is the totally private conception that remains in the mind of the one who has it without influencing any act or utterance. For this "public"–"private" distinction it is irrelevant whether the person is consciously aware of having the conception. What matters is whether in some way or other it enters into the domain of the publicly observable. Private conceptions in this sense are not reflected in anything publicly observable, and they are surely extremely rare. Even if there is no conscious awareness of a conception, it is standardly reflected in the person's behavior. But in any case, my focus is only on conceptions that bring with them such public clues.

A DISTORTED PUBLIC SELF

Being subject to distorted conceptions that find some public expression is the common lot of the oppressed. Often the conceptions are not the result of individual malice, but arise from long-standing and socially shared biases. An oppressed person may him/herself reveal a self-conception that is distorted along the same lines. It is no secret that sometimes inappropriately restrictive beliefs and offensive stereotypes are internalized. But whether the victim contributes in this way or not, there can be a pervasive pattern of distortion in the revealed conceptions and images that people have. That is to say, what I call "the public self" of the person—the generally held conception as revealed in a pattern of acts in the surrounding community—is distorted.

Consider, for example, Adrian's attempt to find employment suited to his abilities. If he wears a visible hearing aid, then it seems that his general intelligence is likely to be repeatedly underestimated. This is revealed in the restricted topics of conversation people introduce when with him, in the level of vocabulary, and in the complete disinterest in his views on serious matters even though those around are consulted for theirs. Although not explicitly stated, the shared belief that Adrian is "not very bright" becomes a feature of his public self.

Or consider Estelle, the lone woman employee in a small workplace, who quickly realizes that any indignation or anger is automatically characterized by her coworkers as "emotional hysteria," legitimate concern is described as "anxiety," and if she is very careful about something in a perfectly rational way, she is labelled as "obsessive." She is never consulted about difficult problems that need a cool head to solve, and there are sporadic jokes about the irrationality of women. In short, Estelle learns that her public self, as shared by her coworkers, includes the characterization of her as irrational, emotional, and unstable.

The acts of many people may be relevant to the public self in question. With a less specific example, Sandra Bartky notes that:

> Innocent chatter, the currency of ordinary social life, or a compliment ("You don't think like a woman"), the well-intentioned advice of psychologists, the news item, the joke, the cosmetics advertisement. . . . Each reveals itself, depending on the circumstances in which it appears, as a threat, an insult, an affront, as a reminder, however subtle, that I belong to an inferior caste.[19]

It is relevant to my focus on nonviolent oppression that all of the items Bartky cites are seemingly mundane and trivial matters. The significance of the pattern, however, is far from trivial. Large numbers of people are involved in the construction of the public self here precisely because she is referring to a member of one large group of oppressed people, namely, women. So whatever particularities the public self includes with respect to this or that woman, it often includes the negative components attributed to women in general.

Since the public self of a person is community specific, it is quite possible for a person to have two or more different public selves by belonging to more than one community. Since Chris is unemployed and homeless, his public self in the community at large includes strongly negative features from the associated stereotypes, such as being lazy, rude, and dangerous. Among the local street people, however, Chris is more accurately known and his public self includes features like being active and ingenious, being trustworthy and a safe person to call upon when threatened.

When there is more than one public self, there is no guarantee, of course, that any one of them will be reasonably accurate. The public self, after all, is a construct, and it may or may not be based on unbiased observation and interaction. Also it is possible that it is fairly accurate only because it has had a crucial contributory role in molding the person in question. In these cases the public self itself influences the development of the person's character and attributes, at least for a considerable time. Children who are openly and brutally described as "stupid" usually perform down to the level of general expectation, even those time will reveal to be exceptionally intelligent.

THE INTRACTABILITY OF THE DISTORTIONS

There are at least two factors that help explain the intractable nature of the distorted conceptions. One has to do with a form of power that the privileged have in abundance, and the other concerns a support mechanism that protects errors about public selves.

Victims of negatively distorted public selves are usually powerless to have them changed. This claim will seem implausible to many in positions of privilege and security. After all, if no physical force or threat of it is being used, and there are no laws embodying the objectionable public self, then where lies the problem? Surely the people concerned can correct any misconceptions if they are articulate and accurate themselves?

This reflects an unrealistic but not unusual view of how daily interactions are managed in our society. If we are speaking about people who are peers with respect to power and status, then it is a fair comment, but those at the receiving end of oppression have far less power and status than the agents responsible. And as we have seen, the different kinds of power involved in daily interactions include far more than are generally acknowledged, and this is crucial in understanding why the distorted public selves of the oppressed are so intractable.

We have already noted that a privileged person typically has what I describe as indirect power, power that arises via the roles and actions of third parties. Also much of the direct power enjoyed by the privileged goes beyond any legitimately assigned power attached to any social role. This is especially true of interactive power, and inappropriate power of this kind is particularly prone to distort interactions and block accurate knowledge of the more vulnerable.

Since in the kinds of cases I am looking at the preconceptions are entrenched, socially accepted, and often without malice, they tend not to be dislodged by simply "seeing" the people in question and seeing that the preconceptions are biased. It typically requires sustained and focused communication of one sort or another, most of it, in the initial stages anyway, from articulate victims. This in turn means that the relatively powerless people who are subject to the construction of distorted public selves need to be able to initiate contacts (like conversations), speak freely, object to the misconceptions, insist on being listened to, and so on. In short, they need at least as much interactive power as the privileged who may be contributing to and sustaining those distortions. And this is not the case.

AN ERROR-PROTECTING MECHANISM

The second factor that makes distorted public selves so hard to correct is the existence of at least one support mechanism that sustains and reinforces errors. It is not that those holding the misconceptions are unusually stubborn as individuals but, rather, that the social construct of a person's prestige value is often at work. Like other social constructs, prestige requires community involvement. One individual cannot establish or sustain the prestige of anything. It depends on the attitudes of many people.

Also prestige is community specific, just like a person's public self. Someone or something may be prestigious within one community but have no such standing within another. In nineteenth-century England a rich industrialist may have had prestige within merchant society, but that by no means ensured him the same standing within aristocratic circles. In fact in that period many of the "landed gentry" had contempt for those whose wealth came from "trade." This example also reminds us that the nature of a community's involvement can change over time. Although remants of the traditional attitude can be found, members of the aristocracy in England now accord a lot more prestige value to those whose wealth comes from business activities and, indeed, some members of titled families have moved into business activities themselves.

The communities involved can vary in size, but some people have prestige within society at large. In Western societies today they usually include members of certain professions, such as lawyers, clergy, architects, doctors. Professionally senior members, like judges, generals, and bishops, have even higher standing.

On the other hand, others may suffer the assignment of close to zero prestige value in society at large, including the poor, the unemployed, members of ethnic minorities, the physically or mentally challenged, and more. It is true that any individual in these groups may also be a member of a more specifc community, like a political organization or a church, and be accorded a high prestige value there. But it is not unusual for the prestige value that holds at the societal level (such as the high prestige attached to certain professions or the low prestige attached to being poor and unemployed) to carry through to the person's standing within smaller, more specifically focused communities. The wider societal perspective often dominates. Quite often it is the parishioners who are members of the high-status professions who are made church wardens.

As recently as 1986 we can read in a philosophy article on dignity (by Zbigniew Szawarksi) that "by the mere fact of doing some specific job or fulfilling some social role—being a judge, a statesman or ecclesiastic—the person involved acquires a special right to be respected."[20] This contains no explicit reference to "prestige," but it captures the flavor of how prestigious occupations function within social relationships. The danger is surely obvious. This kind of sweeping claim about the "special" status of individuals in certain social roles throws a protective veil over even the outright malicious judge, politician, or priest. It is one of the reasons why some priests, for example, have been able to sexually abuse children for a decade or more completely unscathed and without being confronted by any adult. If one or two of the victims try to report the outrages to another adult, it is not unusual for the reports to be indignantly dismissed without inquiry, especially if the adult is not a parent of the victim. The very idea of a member of the clergy being involved in such behavior is an affront to the listener's long-standing respect for the role. One can sympathize with this. After all, we ought to be able to count on priests and ministers being guiltless of such serious immorality, no matter what small human failings of the usual kind they have. Nonetheless, it remains true that this pattern functions to protect the corrupt priest.

In fact high prestige functions protectively for those who have it in more ways than one. In nearly every community or organization, someone with high prestige can often "get away with" things that a lower prestige person could not. The sense in which the person can "get away with it" is often a strong sense: some omission or blunder or error of judgment can occur blatantly and in front of other people and yet it simply is not seen. The predisposition to see excellence is so strong that the perception of excellence is imposed on whatever actually happens. This is the well known "emperor's new clothes" phenomenon, and it differs from the case mentioned above where the problem is concealed in a more literal sense and where the child-abuse victim cannot get adults to investigate the actions of the priest.

The "emperor's new clothes" phenomenon occurs not only with respect to an occasional lapse, but sometimes in a more sinister way. Most of us have at some time or other encountered people whose high prestige is altogether inexplicable on rational grounds. How could this rise to prominence happen? How could an unreliable, closed-minded, racist lawyer ever rise to a prestigious position as a judge? How could a self-serving, arrogant, duplicitous priest ever come to be a bishop? Such individuals should never be placed in those roles, but if different groups of people are involved at different stages of their advancement, it is not so difficult to understand. Suppose that the applicant to law school has borderline grades but is well known as the son of a famous criminal court lawyer, so he is accepted because of his mother's prestige. He steers close to the most prestigious faculty during his studies so that, although his achievements are modest, he has prestigious names as references. Family connections ensure that he is hired by an old and famous law firm. And so it goes on. How could his racism not hinder his career? He always works with and associates with others who, like himself, are white and who take racist jokes as just an expression of humor. Significantly, when exposure eventually occurs in these kinds of cases, it is often at the hands of someone who is *not* a member of the relevant community, in this case, the legal profession. As the biologist R. C. Lewontin notes in commenting on the relationship between judgments of the merit of academic work and the prestige of academic institutions, "Despite the claim that in the marketplace of ideas it is the better-made product that wins the consumer's heart, it is, in fact, brand loyalty that counts. 'Made in Cambridge' [i.e., Harvard] has always been worth far more than the force of logic.''[21]

Of course, not only does high prestige tend to mask even major inadequacies but also low prestige tends to conceal exceptionally desirable attributes. People with low prestige tend to be on a downward spiral, since it leaves them stranded and excluded, and the increasing marginalization robs them of what little prestige value they may have left. This greatly affects both their credibility and how their desirable attributes are perceived—or more to the point, not perceived.

It is not surprising that these dangers are more easily seen by those with low prestige than by those with high prestige, and sometimes one can find an unrealistic level of optimism about such matters. For example, in *Justice and the Human Good*, William Galston writes about what he calls "public honor" and claims that "a system of public honor tends to . . . reduce hypocrisy and increase the unity and integrity of the community," and that "honor does not pervert virtue or excellence as readily as does material reward."[22] There are relevant analogies between public honor and prestige, but Galston displays no awareness of how they actually function and the dangers they present for self-corruption and inappropriate relationships.

There *are* people who see beyond someone's prestige value, and within some professions a few small changes have been aimed at checking the clearly unfair advantages sometimes attached to high prestige. (For example, some academic journals remove the author's name before an article is reviewed.) In the main, however, Western societies place a much higher value on prestige than on merit alone, and the two do not always coincide. Since prestige value is typically included in the person's public self, the strong reluctance to significantly demote or promote means that we leave uncorrected some seriously flawed public selves. Also, any misconceived public selves functioning in the minds and actions of those with high prestige are particularly unlikely to be corrected. The very fact that these conceptions are accepted by those with such social status protects the errors, since the privileged are less likely to be effectively challenged by the less powerful (as we have already noted) and since it is understandable if the privileged do not self-correct the errors when those errors favor their higher social status. The role of a person's prestige value, then, helps sustain and reinforce seriously distorted public selves.

COERCION AND CONTROL

We usually think of coercion as a form of control involving either direct intervention or threats of violence, economic deprivation, or something

similar. That is to say, it works by holding up a vision of dire consequences for those who do not comply. But there can indeed be very effective control without anything that looks like coercion. We already have
one example of this in the way that put-down humor usually functions
when initiated by the more privileged and secure. The victims may have
no way to object without socially "causing a scene," with all the predictable embarrassment that involves. Their objections disrupt the social
scene precisely because they disrupt the submissive and compliant relationships so often unconsciously taken as owing to the more privileged.
The victims are also likely to be shunned because they are "poor sports"
or "have no sense of humor." So they usually "comply" with the joke.
But for most participants and observers, there is nothing in all this that
would count as coercion—or threats of it. Yet if the put-down content embodies a badly distorted public self, then repeated use of the jokes can
sustain that negative image. The public self can then block recognition of
important favorable attributes the victims have. That in turn constrains
the interactions between the victims and those subscribing to the public
self, nearly always to the detriment of the victims.

Also, another form of control that does not involve threats is very effective, especially in its long-term consequences. It consists in "the refusal to
engage." This can only work well as a form of control when in the hands
of privileged and secure members of society. A refusal to engage,
whether that refusal is conscious or not, is easily sustained given the vast
discrepancy in interactive power between the privileged and oppressed.
And this refusal leaves its victims unable to function as they should, and
leaves negative distortions in their public selves uncorrected. These restrictions naturally bring with them a general lack of awareness of the
victims' perspective and the kinds of accounts and insights that might
lead to a more adequate conceptualization of day-to-day oppression. This
refusal to engage is radically different from the "noninterference" that
promotes basic freedom among peers.

Sandra Lee Bartky writes in *Femininity and Domination* that "oppression
. . . is ordinarily conceived in too limited a fashion" and that "this has
placed undue restrictions both on our understanding of what oppression
itself is and on the categories of persons we might want to classify as oppressed."[23] This I heartily agree with. Indeed, Bartky's book develops one
insight after another. But there is one place where an oversight appears
to be at work. In describing categories or types of oppression, the options
Bartky offers seem themselves to be too limited. She writes: "It is possible
to be oppressed in ways that need involve neither physical deprivation,
legal inequality, nor economic exploitation; one can be oppressed psychologically . . . [which] can be regarded as the 'internalization of intimations
of inferiority.' "[24] But this moves too quickly from "not oppressed physi-

cally, legally, or economically" to "internally oppressed," and omits other forms of oppression that are external to the victim. One of these I have tried to articulate here, namely, the power-backed refusal to engage. It may, but by no means need, involve internalized oppression on the part of the victims. And given the distorted public selves and the role of interactive power, it certainly is a form of control, and one that the relatively powerless can do little about except in the very long run. And so, I contend, it is an effective form of oppression, since oppression has at its heart systematic and morally inappropriate control embedded in relationships that are morally unacceptable.

And this is where one of the great myths about oppression breaks down, since this control devastates what should be the proper moral relations and can indeed seriously distort the lives of those concerned without any dramatic, highly visible malicious or brutal acts being involved. Disempowerment and unjust exclusion on a scale that can wreck lives often arise via a relentless series of inappropriate but tiny interventions and omissions, none of them maliciously intended, and most of them entirely unnoticed by the agents. And the process is not only cumulative in itself, but compounded by the error-protecting role of the relative social prestige.

Consequential power, support power, and overgeneralized interactive power, all commonplace for privileged people, play a largely unseen role in various relationships, and all sometimes contribute to civilized oppression. Since the socially privileged have these types of power in abundance with little or no awareness of them, anyone so privileged has an obligation to explore what is involved, especially by listening to articulate people at the receiving end of such power. As Laurence Thomas writes in his article "Moral Deference,"

> It is a mode of moral learning which those who have been oppressed are owed in the name of eliminating the very state of their oppression. In the absence of such learning, oppression cannot but continue to be a part of the fabric of the moral life. Indeed, the . . . studied refusal to engage in such learning is one of the very ways in which oppression manifests itself.[25]

Civilized oppression will not be reduced if it is not approached as a mutual endeavor involving both the more powerful and the more vulnerable. We need more adequate concepts of power, and an analysis of hidden power, in our own relationships and in social structures on the large scale. We need to beware naive concepts of power that assume that "assigned power" denotes privilege. We need the perceptual skills to spot both patterns and specific incidents of power misuse, and we will need to work with rigorous honesty to curtail all the many generally accepted slides into inappropriate uses of power. It requires better insights into the role of social prestige, and an active resistance to its compounding effect on oppressive marginalization, but we need also to beware of dangerously oversimplified 'solutions' where inappropriate and easily abused power is simply removed from one group and transferred to another. We need to build communication mechanisms so that people under the scope of our power can raise any concerns at an early stage, request or be offered information they are entitled to, and be themselves to the extent that they are as well known as they should be. And we will need to explore the moral foundations of basically sound relationships that happen to involve nonpeers (something we will look at later in this work). These kinds of things are not achieved by a pure heart and gritted teeth, but only by sustained work, much of which, as we have seen, must first be tackled on the conceptual and the moral levels.[26]

NOTES

1. Judith Andre, "Power, Oppression and Gender," *Social Theory and Practice* 11, no. 1 (Spring 1985): 107–22, 114.

2. For example, John Rawls, *A Theory of Justice* (Cambridge, Mass.: Harvard University Press, 1971); David Miller, *Social Justice* (Oxford: Clarendon Press, 1976); William A. Galston, *Justice and the Human Good* (Chicago: University of Chicago Press, 1980); Bruce A. Ackerman, *Social Justice in the Liberal State* (New Haven, Conn.: Yale University Press, 1980).

3. Iris Marion Young, "Displacing the Distributive Paradigm," chapter 1 in *Justice and the Politics of Difference* (Princeton, N.J.: Princeton University Press, 1990).

4. Young, 9.

5. Since writing this, I have been delighted to find in Christine M. Koggel's recent book, *Perspectives on Equality* (Lanham, Md.: Rowman & Littlefield, 1998), an impressive study of issues concerning equality and justice analyzed in terms of relationships. Her work on relationships of unequal power and their social and political implications converges to some degree with my study of civilized oppression.

6. Andre, 117.

7. Andre, 118.

8. Andre, 118.

9. Andre, 119.

10. Thomas E. Wartenberg, *The Forms of Power* (Philadelphia: Temple University Press, 1990), 141.

11. Wartenberg, 145.

12. Wartenberg, 146.

13. Wartenberg, 145.

14. Wartenberg, 156.

15. Wartenberg, 156.

16. Wartenberg, 156.

17. Wartenberg, 155.

18. Marilyn Frye, *The Politics of Reality* (Freedom, Calif.: Crossing Press, 1983), 47.

19. Sandra Lee Bartky, *Femininity and Domination* (New York: Routledge, 1990), 17.

20. Zbigniew Szawarksi, "Dignity and Responsibility," *Dialectics and Humanism* 13, no. 2–3 (Spring/Summer, 1986): 193–205, 193.

21. R. C. Lewontin, "Women Versus the Biologists," *The New York Review of Books*, 7 April 1994: 31–35, 33.

22. William A. Galston, *Justice and the Human Good* (Chicago: University of Chicago Press, 1980), 274.

23. Bartky, 29.

24. Bartky, 22.

25. Laurence Thomas, "Moral Deference," *Philosophical Forum* 24, no. 1–3 (Fall/Spring 1992–93): 233–50, 247.

26. Since reaching this conclusion, I have come upon Margaret Urban Walker's wide-ranging new book on the current state of moral philosophy, *Moral Understandings* (New York: Routledge, 1998). In chapter 8, "Unnecessary Identities: Representational Practices and Moral Recognition," she remarks that "analysis of privileged or malicious constructions of social identity is standard fare in burgeoning literatures of cultural, literary, feminist, and ethnographic studies, and theories of race, postcolonialism, and sexuality. What is startling is how little attention has been paid to this at the centre of moral philosophy 'proper' " (180). She adds, "I hope only to make persuasive the claim that moral graphics and the politics of representation, which have scarcely been topics in moral philosophy at all, are among its most urgent issues" (181). On this we concur. The matters I have discussed in this chapter, like the forms of "relationship power" and the role of "the public self," are central to moral theory and should be recognized as such.

Chapter 4

On the Receiving End

In this chapter I will look more closely at the situation of victims, examining particularly the relationships of unequal power that are standardly involved in civilized oppression. One way to explore the implications of the imbalance of power is to consider what issues arise once someone has been wronged. What recourse does the victim have? Can the victim protest or not, and how will protest affect the ultimate outcome? Should third parties intervene? By attending to the situation of the victims and the relative power in the relationships, we will uncover new ways in which the imbalance of power continues to operate.

PEER VERSUS NONPEER RELATIONSHIPS

Suppose Ruth borrows Ann's text for an hour, promising to return it, since Ann needs it to finish a paper due the next morning. Instead Ruth goes to a party, locking the book in her room. If they are both students and neither has any special status, then we would expect Ann's justifiable anger to be expressed to Ruth in no uncertain terms. She may do so even if she learns from other friends that Ruth uses people in this kind of fashion all the time and that no amount of protesting results in any change.

This is a simple example of the classic person-to-person wrong between two peers: the agent and victim have much the same overall power and social status, before and after the wrong. It is the most promising candidate for a kind of situation where there is no obligation for any third person to protest. But the main reason is not the futility of doing so (in that the wrong is over before protest is an option, and the agent will not change future behavior, and so on). If there is no obligation, it is because the person with the foremost moral right to protest, namely, the victim, is ex hypothesi fully empowered to do so and is dealing with an individual who is a peer.

But even prior to any wrongdoing, many relationships are those of nonpeers, involving either natural differences in power, such as those between a young child and her parent (such as the difference in physical and intellectual capacities); or socially constructed differences, such as those holding between most black American males and most white American males (such as in achievable income); or the difference between the rich and the poor (in many respects, such as in political lobbying power, in day-to-day comfort); or the difference between a military recruit and the general staff (such as in their knowledge of battle plans). Such constructed differences may or may not be morally justified. Many are not.

Even if two people are in a peer relationship prior to the wrongdoing, some acts of wrongdoing make former peers nonpeers in some fairly ongoing way. The most extreme cases are where the wrong leaves the victim dead or incapacitated in long-term ways, either physically or mentally. But there are other serious if less drastic ways where a wrong changes a peer relationship into that of nonpeers, such as if one employee misrepresents another so that the latter loses her position.

A victim is entitled to protest a wrong, that is, to point out the wrong to those responsible and to object to it and the harm involved. Doing so draws attention to the wrong and the harm it involves and makes clear that they matter to the victim. Whether the wrong is explicitly intended or not, or whether the agent is culpable or not, are not crucial issues here. What matters most is the sheer fact that there is something that should not have been, with someone at the receiving end. A lack of moral culpability does not excuse us from concern about serious moral wrongs where we are the agents, and it is prima facie appropriate to amend something that should not have happened in the first place and to work out how to reduce the likelihood of our repeating the wrong in the future.

DISEMPOWERED VICTIMS

In cases of wrongs involving nonpeers, however, the victim is sometimes not fully empowered to register a protest, and there are at least four common ways in which this can occur. In the first place there may be a *material impossibility*. In practice it is impossible for the victim to protest. Perhaps the victim is a very young child or an animal, unable to articulate a clearly intelligible protest. Or the person is imprisoned in total isolation, never allowed out of his dark cell, allowed no verbal contact with anyone—like the most shocking recorded cases of solitary confinement. Or perhaps the wrong is completely unforeseeable and afterwards the victim is dead or has lost the necessary capacities for protest.

Even if the victim is aware and articulate, there may be, secondly, the *retaliation response*. When a protest is made, the victim is attacked or further harmed in some major way. Or thirdly, there is *constrained silence*. The victim remains silent because a protest *would* result in retaliation.

In the fourth place there may be the practical equivalent of silencing via a *total nonresponse* so that, so far as genuinely registering a protest is concerned, there is no difference at all between the victim's having spoken and having remained silent. In the worst cases some institutions have deliberately set up sessions where employees can "let off steam" about their serious concerns, but all with complete futility. It is well known that as time passes, this treatment usually demoralizes those with concerns and they cease even trying to protest. We should beware at this point of the all too tempting suggestion that the victims should "demand" a response, since that very language makes sense only if they have some kind of clout with which to press the issue. The inconvenient or embarrassing "demands" of the powerless, no matter how articulate, perceptive, or fairly reasoned, quite standardly fall on deaf ears. As Bernard Boxill bluntly points out, "people do not take the powerless seriously."[1] Being powerless in the sense referred to here is of course context dependent. It includes far more than those whose individual attributes leave them unable to communicate a protest. Indeed, very articulate, strong-minded, and perceptive people can be powerless with respect to some specific situation they are in, usually because of the nature of the relationships involved.

With the last three of these types of victim disempowerment, distorted nonpeer relationships are usually at work. There are many day-to-day examples of such disempowerment. Articulate older children in authoritarian schools bear unjust treatment from teachers in silence, since the price of protesting is to be unfairly targeted in a long-term way as a "troublemaker." Recruits in the military share the same type of experience in basic training. This kind of retaliation response is all too familiar in news items and documentaries. Also there are cases where a woman protests sexual harassment by an employment supervisor, only to suffer greater hostility and harassment in retaliation. This in turn results in other women remaining silent about the abuse they receive. They live in constrained silence. Again, in many places in the world a man in poverty may find work only in an unregulated workplace where any worker who even mentions unsafe conditions or unfair procedures is immediately fired and blacklisted. In some places this means starvation for the worker and the worker's family. Most financially desperate employees remain silent in such conditions. In more industrialized countries miners have sometimes protested about some safety issue, been told "it will be looked into," and then discovered that this amounted to absolutely nothing. If this is a noticeable pattern of response and if this is the only work available in the area, protests gradually subside in the face of such transparent and total nonresponse.

It is easy to oversimplify what is involved in an institution's ensuring some genuine recourse for those it wrongs (whether culpably or not). In particular it cannot be equated with the institution's having formal procedures for grievances or appeals. In many institutions such procedures have been set up in good faith and with the best of intentions, but quite a few of those responsible for this have not seen, let alone eliminated, the actual threats and penalties directed to those who try to use them. There is in fact considerable naïveté in some conceptions of what is involved in victim-initiated recourse in the face of actual or imminent injustice at the hands of powerful agents. Furthermore, even if the procedures are successfully called upon, it is not uncommon for the victim to be left without any adequate redress, although vindicated, so to speak, by the acknowledgment of wrong.

For example, suppose a person applies for a "higher level" employment position and is rejected in favor of someone else who has fewer qualifications. Even if it is eventually established that this is unfair and is the result of, say, ageism or racism or sexism, the outcome may still be far from adequate. In most places there is no requirement, either legally or via institutional regulations, to release the person already hired. In fact, in most places, it cannot legally be done. The piece of injustice is treated as a fait accompli with no possible reversal. The person who should have been hired may receive some minor financial compensation (not even close to the years of earnings that would have been received in the position applied for), and sometimes some assurance of being "considered" next time a similar position opens up. That assurance amounts to very little if there is unlikely to be another such position open in the foreseeable future. The very fact that the best outcome is morally inadequate in this kind of way functions as a deterrent to calling upon the grievance procedures. Also, some institutions have set up procedures because of external pressure and solely for the sake of public appearance. In such cases there may be no real commitment to them. These are institutions where the leadership objects deeply to challenges to the institution's power-backed decision. For example, if it is established that someone was unfairly rejected for a position, then the assurance of being "considered" next time amounts to nothing at all in such an institution, since the victim will be "considered" as a "trouble-maker" in the future and will not be hired. The only change in such a case will be that the institutional agents will be far more careful in just how the person is rejected. In the very worst kind of case, an institution may adopt appeal procedures so resentfully that explicit thought is given as to how to nullify them.

Having formal appeal procedures, then, by no means ensures there is some genuine recourse for those the institution wrongs. According to reports, there have been cases in Western countries where women in the military have protested sexual harassment on the part of a supervisor and were then subjected to extended hostility, pressure, and harassment as "a trouble-maker" from others on the base. Sometimes outright threats were received. Again, news documentaries have reported that some women in police forces who have protested sexual harassment by male supervisors have been shunned and reviled, and they have been made the targets of every conceivable fault-finding move in the book. Relentless hostile scrutiny is of course a form of harassment. In a number of these kinds of cases the woman has been so badly savaged and betrayed during the lengthy grievance process that she has been unable to continue in her chosen career. She was in the classic "no win" situation and would suffer unjustly whether she protested or remained silent. Whether it involved an innocent lack of awareness, a willful lack of awareness, or something worse, there being formal procedures in no way safeguarded fair treatment of the women, and the illusion of their providing a just outcome when wronged was quickly demolished.

The correlation between genuine recourse and formal procedures fails in the other direction also. Although not common, there can be institutions, usually rather small, with no formal procedures for protest or appeal, but where protests can be raised—and to the most appropriate person, the alleged wrongdoer—without further harm, and where such protests are reflected upon with an open mind.

TWO WRONGS, NOT ONE

In the rest of this chapter I will focus on one large set of cases, namely, where *the wrongdoer is an institutional agent, the victim is articulate and aware, but has far less power and status, and where one or another of the last three types of victim disempowerment above is at work,* that is, retaliation response, constrained silence, or total nonresponse. In these cases the victim, as an individual, has the kinds of personal attributes needed to articulate a protest, so protest is not materially impossible. (All the above examples are of one of these kinds.)

If we have disempowerment of any of these three kinds, then where we may seem to have one wrong, we in fact clearly have at least two. There is the original wrong (the injustice to the pupil or army recruit, the sexual harassment, or the unnecessarily dangerous work conditions) and then there is the wrong of blocking legitimate protest by the victims. And, of course, if in protesting the original wrong one experiences either total nonresponse or retaliation, then one is unlikely to proceed to protest the second wrong—that of having the original protest blocked. Ex hypothesi, it is not materially impossible for the victim to protest either wrong, but protest is blocked nonetheless and this signals something important about the relationship between the victim and whoever is responsible for the blocking (usually some person or group within the institution in the first instance).

What I suggest about this relationship is that it is oppressive, and although far from inevitable, it is nonetheless in the nature of the case that oppression of this kind can persist for a long time without being seen by people of good will in privileged positions. An alert third party may observe the original wrong, such as the unnecessary safety hazard in the workplace or the unfair berating of the military recruit, and may even observe the retaliation or the total nonresponse when the victim protests. But it is much harder to perceive the ongoing nature of the inappropriate relationship, what I refer to as "victim oppression," and there are several reasons why. The first two reasons are the most important philosophically, since they have to do with the nature of oppressive relationships.

WHY VICTIM OPPRESSION IS A LESS VISIBLE HARM

The first reason it is difficult to perceive victim oppression has to do with *what it takes to reveal this relationship.* To begin with, in some oppressive situations it can take just one serious case of effective retaliation inflicted on a protester, or a handful of cases of total nonresponse, for the protest suppression to be revealed to the victims. In the kinds of situations we are looking at, the one incident of serious retaliation or the few cases of nonresponse reveal the ongoing and morally inappropriate relationship at work. Institutional agents who standardly suppress victim protest, even unconsciously, in effect use their power as a control mechanism over those the institution wrongs. When the incidents are over, the oppression remains if the oppressive relationship remains. For obvious reasons the victims directly involved in the incidents tend to remain aware of the ongoing oppressive relationship when the incidents are over, aware that they are being inappropriately controlled and are unable in any practical sense to do what they are entitled to do, namely, protest in some meaningful way when wronged. These are not simply one or two unpleasant incidents now in the past. They tell the victims something about their whole future so long as they are in that same situation, since the incidents make them aware of their relative powerlessness even with respect to future wrongs. So they are living with a kind of vulnerability that is avoidable and immoral, and that tends to erode both their self-respect and their day-to-day confidence in life, at least if the institution is important to them.

It is very easy for those not on the receiving end of this to be simply unaware of the ongoing nature of the problem, especially if the inappropriate relationship is not the result of explicit intent. Morally inappropriate relationships certainly tend to result in tangible harm to the victims, but in the first place this is not logically guaranteed, and second, when there is straightforwardly tangible harm, it may be sporadic even though the distorted relationship is ongoing. This in fact is one of the important features of an oppressive relationship—that it can persist after any easily visible acts of harm are over.[2]

The second reason that victim oppression is not easily seen is that *the scope of the victim-group* is often understandably misjudged. The victims of the oppressive relationship include far more than those people who actually protest and then experience retaliation or nonresponse. If one worker is fired from an unregulated workplace because he voices concern about an unnecessary safety hazard, not only is he unfairly treated, but his fellow workers receive a very clear message, in fact, a threat. They are all in an ongoing oppressive relationship whether or not they actually protest and actually lose their employment because of it. In the kind of case we are looking at, what happens to the one worker reveals the morally inappropriate relationship holding not just between him and the employer, but between the employer and all the workers there: they are all being oppressively controlled. Again this is an important feature of an oppressive relationship—that one can be subjected to it in an ongoing way without ever being the recipient of the most likely, associated, tangible harm. And again, this makes the full scope of the victim-group hard to detect by those whose lives are free of it.

In the third place it is relevant to mention *the seriousness of the wrong*. I suspect that this can be established best experientially, not in print, but contrary to the traditional "scientific" ethos, this makes the actual point all the more crucial to state. Even if the full scope of the victim-group is acknowledged, there will be a predictable tendency on the part of those not trapped in such ongoing oppressive relationships to underestimate the seriousness of the day-to-day harm and misery involved, especially if we are referring to victims who have not protested and so have not personally received the foreseeable and morally inappropriate response (for example, did not protest the dangerous work-conditions and so were not fired). In addition to the harm of the original wrong (the dangerous conditions), to be fully alert in such a situation is to be "weighted down" day after day by the degrading phenomenon of being immorally controlled and unfairly treated, and to be dismally aware of having no effective power in the case of any future mistreatment or injustice. It is among other things a very demoralizing type of wrong, since in its classic form there is no foreseeable escape, except to be further harmed. For these reasons, even when observers become aware of the the scope of the victim oppression, they remain unaware of how serious the matter is, especially in the case of victims who are not actually recipients of the overtly immoral response.

A fourth reason that victim oppression is hard to detect is that we *overestimate the effectiveness of the victims' personal attributes*. When we ask if some individual is "powerless" or not, it is easy to blur the distinction between personal attributes and situational factors and to place far too heavy an emphasis on personal attributes. We think of someone who is very articulate, perceptive, clear thinking, and calmly assertive as anything but a powerless individual. Yet many such people are rendered powerless by oppressive structures. The individual attributes are standardly an inadequate defense against oppression. In fact, to be realistic, many such individuals are targeted and rendered powerless by institutional agents precisely because their personal attributes make them potentially serious advocates for those the institution wrongs.

A further reason that victim oppression is less visible concerns the fact that *a lot of it is unconscious*. Even the targeting of potential advocates is often without explicit intent, and it is hard for us to become aware of the wrongs we commit or support habitually or unconsciously. Good will alone is not enough. We need an adequate conceptual apparatus to inform our reflection and perceptions, and in addition we need perceptual skills that are developing in an ongoing fashion. Acquiring the intellectual insights by no means provides a person with the ability to spot the relevant incidents and patterns. Usually such perceptual skills are acquired slowly, over years. Also, given that various forms of oppression have survived for centuries at the hands of privileged people of good will, it seems that neither an adequate conceptual apparatus nor the relevant perceptual skills just naturally arise in the course of a person's life. They involve effort and commitment.

The final reason I will mention here is that *victim oppression is often nonmaliciously self-perpetuating* when it is unconscious, since it silences the most valuable source of insight, namely, articulate and aware recipients of it. If an institutional structure is unconsciously functioning in this way, then privileged institutional members full of good will may well never become aware of it, since it is precisely that kind of communication from the least powerful that is being suppressed.

COMMONSENSE VIEW ON THIRD-PARTY PROTEST

These are serious obstacles to seeing oppressive relationships clearly. They therefore pose moral dangers to those who may be implicated without realizing it, and many contributory agents are indeed unaware of their involvement. But let us consider now the relationship between victims and third parties or spectators, who, however, *are* aware of the wrongs. They are aware of the original wrong and they can see the victim oppression, the suppression of meaningful, victim-initiated protest about that original wrong. Being witness to such oppressive relationships, the question arises as to whether they should intervene by protesting on behalf of the victim. To locate the issues involved in this question about third-party protest, it will help to consider the controversial response of the Roman Catholic Church to the barbaric oppression of the Holocaust. But first we should be a little clearer about what constitutes a "third party."

There are various ways of being complicitous in a moral wrong, such as being *fairly directly involved in bringing it about*—as was Eichmann in the murder of European Jews, or *sustaining those more directly involved*—by providing money or personnel, or more personally, by providing vital encouragement or by freeing up time and energy by providing meals and general day-to-day care. As well as helping to bring about the wrong, one can *capitalize on the wrong*—like those who made money by manufacturing gas for murdering Jews. One can also *compound the harm* to the victim, something often motivated by hostility rather than by personal gain—like the extreme brutality used in force-feeding the English suffragettes imprisoned early in the twentieth century. Or one can be in a position to *prevent any of the above* and yet not do so.

Suppose that one is not the victim of some wrong, nor complicitous in the wrong in the any of the above kinds of ways. Suppose, that is, that one is a "third party." Suppose further that protesting will not prevent the kinds of complicity mentioned above: it will not stop any of those fairly directly involved in bringing about the wrong; it will not change any of those who are sustaining those more directly involved, or who are capitalizing on the wrong; it will have no effect on those who are compounding the wrong; and it will not goad out of their inertia those who *could* effectively prevent some of these things. Furthermore, protesting will not bring about redress for the victim, nor effect any reform in the wrongdoer(s) or other potential wrongdoers which would prevent a future wrong. As a shorthand I will refer to this as "an unfavorable situation for protesting" or as simply "an unfavorable situation" if the rest is clear from the context.

Sometimes *nothing* one can do as a third party will bring about any of the desirable effects above, and this I will call "a totally unfavorable situation" and will not abbreviate it further. Obviously an unfavorable situation for protesting need not be totally unfavorable, since there may be some other course of action that would be far more effective than protesting.

If one is a third party, is there any prima facie obligation to protest a wrong in an unfavorable situation for protesting? What I call the classic justification for denying any such obligation is exemplified by Cardinal Montini (who later became Paul VI) in his defense of Pope Pius XII. According to Hannah Arendt in "The Deputy: Guilt by Silence?" during World War II Pope Pius XII never publicly protested against the Holocaust, not even when Jews were being taken from Rome, and Montini, in referring to this silence, argues that "An attitude of protest and condemnation . . . would have been not only futile but harmful; that is the long and the short of the matter."[3] "Futile" here means that the murders will not be stopped, reduced, or delayed, in response to a protest. If in addition protesting will not prevent the attached secondary wrongs, nor help to reform the wrongdoers, and so on, if, indeed, we assume that the situation really is unfavorable for protesting, then futility alone seems sufficient to eliminate any obligation to protest, without looking at its being potentially "harmful." Yet I believe that as a general position, this is seriously flawed.

Different issues arise depending on whether a protest would be simply "futile" or actually harmful. In particular, the issues are complicated if protest by a third party would bring further harm to the victims (although if such a protest is self-initiated, this result is not so likely). In any case, I can reach the most crucial moral points I have in mind just by considering situations where protest would be futile (but not harmful), and I will argue that sometimes we have a prima facie obligation to protest even in such circumstances.

Also, I am considering only genuine protest, that is protest that is sincere and not self-deceptive, since the traditional view I am referring to has that same focus. The latter view argues that third-person protest, even when sincere and not self-deceptive, has no moral justification in an unfavorable situation (except perhaps as an expression of moral integrity, which I look at below).

CONTRIBUTING TO UNCERTAIN CONSEQUENTIALIST GOALS

Before setting out my main challenge to the traditional position, some consequentialist challenges of a fairly sophisticated kind should be mentioned. These are justifications that call for acts to be done on principle in apparently unfavorable situations just because they might still contribute to bringing about some desired tangible consequence. (The desired effect may take the form of preventing or lessening something undesirable.)

Typically the desired consequence, in its fullness, is a long way into the future at best, may not be in practice achievable, and has no chance at all of being achieved without many of the relevant acts being performed by many people.

At least three such justifications for protest in apparently futile situations can be given if we consider the effects of general nonprotest in such situations. There are several particularly undesirable consequences that arise if most people accept Montini's position and do not protest.

The first of these is a greater temptation to self-serving self-deception by third parties. Sensible people do not enjoy protesting. It is an unpleasant business at best, and risky at worst. So if we believe that as third parties we have no obligation to protest in an unfavorable situation, then for our own personal comfort or safety we may be tempted to describe a situation as unfavorable when in fact it is not. We may exaggerate anything that already seems to threaten the effectiveness of protest and assume the worst for any factors we know nothing about, all without explicit intent, since the more pessimistic our conclusion, the more entitled we are to remain silent. Then victims may remain without redress or harms may be compounded, when our protest could have prevented such wrongs.

The second undesirable consequence of general nonprotest involves an escalation of power. For fairly obvious reasons most people would rather not hear protests. So if it is generally accepted that third parties have no obligation to protest when the situation is unfavorable for protesting (and a fortiori when it is totally unfavorable), then this may function as an invitation for those in positions or power to *ensure* that protest is futile in all the relevant ways, that is to ensure, so far as possible, that the situations in which protest is likely to arise are in fact unfavorable for protesting, perhaps even totally unfavorable, so that people will have no obligation to protest. Ensuring this is likely to prompt the general cultivation of power and controlling techniques to the level of being overwhelming for at least the most foreseeable targets—the most likely protesters. As with the first consequence, this is something easily done without explicit intent. If there is any awareness at all of the tendency to accumulate power and controlling techniques, it is far more likely to be written into the mental ledger as "forestalling time-consuming interruptions" or "securing a manageable work environment (for oneself)" or something similar. The fact that lack of explicit intent is likely to be a shared feature of both consequences makes them especially intractable.

Both are morally undesirable. The second means there will be more unfavorable situations than there would otherwise have been, and the first means there will be nonprotest in cases where it would be effective in some morally desirable way. One may therefore protest in situations that

are apparently unfavorable just in case it contributes to bringing about
the reduction of these two undesirable consequences.

A third justification that belongs in this category concerns the growing
moral awareness of any society, or more accurately, the lack of it that accompanies general nonprotest. For each society, there are some kinds of
genuine moral wrong not generally perceived. The more basic level of
nonvisibility is when most people have not come to *acknowledge* that
something is morally wrong. They do not believe it and may not even
have thought about it. But there is also a second stage when visibility becomes a problem, at least for many kinds of wrong. This occurs when
there is a general lack of the relevant *perceptual skills*. An intellectual understanding of some fairly subtle kind of wrong does not ensure these
skills. It is disturbingly easy to believe that something is morally wrong
and yet either look at an example of it without recognizing it, or even
worse, unwittingly do it or help others to do it. A good-humored person
may come to believe that sexist jokes are morally objectionable, but this
confers no instant gift of universal detection. It is still possible to laugh at
the traditional "wife jokes" at a marriage reception before realizing that
these denigrating and distorted portrayals of wives and marriage are
sexist.

Where a wrong is generally not seen (because of either of the two problems mentioned above) and the situation is apparently unfavorable, one
may nonetheless protest, even if the agents are nonculpably unaware, just
in case it contributes to raising the visibility of that wrong and others like
it. Cheshire Calhoun, in her paper "Responsibility and Reproach," argues
that outright moral reproach is called for in such contexts,[4] including the
use of "reproachful labels" for the agents, regardless of their culpability.[5]
Again, the goal is to raise the general awareness of the wrong.

But these three justifications remain conseqeuentialist in the standard
sense since they are aiming at a straightforwardly tangible effect. If there
was absolutely no possibility of the effects being achieved, the justifications would collapse. So although important, they do not constitute a
major challenge to the theoretical content of Montini's kind of position.
Such a challenge requires something with a more nonconsequentialist
flavor.

NONCONSEQUENTIALIST APPEAL TO MORAL INTEGRITY

In recent ethical writings few argue that there is any moral point at all in
third-party protest (as distinct from the victim's protesting) in a genuinely unfavorable situation, since ex hypothesi even distant benefits are
not achievable. Perhaps in practice it is never rational to reject the possi-

bility of distant benefits like those mentioned above, but even so, aiming only for distant and very uncertain benefits will typically be eliminated in a utilitarian calculation of the most beneficial act, at least if any nontrivial cost or risk is involved. But in any case we can get to the theoretical question here by asking, *"If* there were no possible benefits of a straightforwardly tangible kind, would there be any grounds at all for third party protest in such unfavorable situations?"

Hannah Arendt is one of the few who challenge the general Montini position by claiming there are such grounds. She writes:

> To be sure, no one can say what actually would have happened had the Pope protested in public. But quite apart from all immediate practical considerations, did no one in Rome realize what so many inside and outside the Church at that time realized, namely, that—in the words of Reinhold Schneider, the late German Catholic writer—a protest against Hitler "would have elevated the Church to a position it has not held since the Middle Ages"?[6]

Arendt's moral assessment is clearly not tied to the practical effects of the protest, but we are not told why protest without such results would "elevate the Church's position," nor what this means. But it is clear that the justification has to do with the potential *protester* (here, the Roman Catholic Church), rather than, for example, the *wrongdoer* or the *victims*. The Pope, after all, as the official representative, would be protesting on behalf of the Roman Catholic Church.

Traditionally there has been one nonconsequentialist justification offered for protesting in an unfavorable situation, and it too focuses on the protester. It calls for the sustaining or expressing of the protester's moral integrity. This appeal is available to Arendt, and certainly any institution publicly claiming to have special "moral authority"—as does the Roman Catholic Church—will correspondingly be expected to maintain moral integrity in an equally visible way. This is a fair expectation regardless of one's view on the claimed moral authority.

A more recent argument for third-party protest is found in Thomas Hill's paper "Symbolic Protest and Calculated Silence." He first rejects several attempted justifications as implausible or not particularly moral, such as protesting for personal satisfaction or protesting as a "minimum form of retribution,"[7] and then he offers a nonconsequentialist justification. He argues that if one has already "associated oneself with [a morally culpable] organization,"[8] then there is some moral point in "disassociating oneself from [serious] evil"[9] it commits, on the grounds that one "cares deeply and genuinely for justice."[10] He writes that " 'Who one is' for moral purposes . . . is determined not simply by substantive contributions to various good or evil causes but to some extent by what and whom

one associates oneself with, and in some contexts this depends importantly on the symbolic gestures one is prepared to make."[11]

Protest here is an expression of the person's moral values and, roughly
speaking, moral integrity. So again it concerns the protester. An appeal
to some form of moral integrity is the one familiar reason cited for third-
party protest in an unfavorable situation, and Hill offers a carefully developed argument in its support. I have no wish to contest Hill on this point.
In fact, if we note the role of what I have called victim oppression in some
institutional wrongs, then his main point about "disassociation" has
added reason to be taken seriously. If, for example, one is a relatively unthreatened member of the institution involved in the wrong and knows
the situation, both the facts about the wrong and the occurrence of victim
oppression, then silence can constitute public support not just of the original wrong but also of this ongoing oppression. Silence can often function
as tacit endorsement in such situations, and it is a kind of complicity in
the oppression. On the other hand, protesting constitutes dissent from the
suppression of the victim's protest by, in a sense, making that suppression as close to pointless as possible. It is a rejection of the institutional
agent's suppression of the victim. This may add yet more significance to
the "disassociation" point, but my main goal in the rest of the chapter is
to offer an additional justification for third-party protest, again, not aimed
at tangible consequences, but that I believe has more moral urgency than
that developed by Hill. This justification is primarily victim focused,
rather than focused on the protester or the wrongdoer.

VICTIM-FOCUSED GROUNDS FOR PROTEST

There is a lot more involved in victim oppression than not allowing the
victim to lodge an objection that should be lodged. There is a sense in
which *publicly* the status of the victim—as *victim*—is being denied by denying the first right of a victim, that of meaningful protest. The victim is
disempowered morally, and usually the victim is blocked in more than
one respect. Typically this can be made to succeed against the morally
sound judgment and will of the victim only if there are major differences
in power and status between the victim and the institutional agent, differences that may be legitimate or natural in themselves but are immorally
used to suppress those the institution wrongs. The recipient is no longer
being accorded an appropriate moral status.

It undermines the person's standing in the part of the moral community the institution embodies, and in a very real sense isolates any individual victim so far as that moral community network is concerned, because
the appropriate relationships within that network have been distorted or

severed. This isolation, of course, is not that of being physically alone. For the alert victim, it brings with it very painful feelings, but the problem itself is not the victim's pain, but rather the nature of the relationships that underlie it, relationships over which the victim has no effective power. One can be complicitous in abandoning the victim to this publicly fabricated, degraded moral status, and this remains true even if one's inner attitude is one of disapproval of the institution's oppressive relationships.

In a totally unfavorable situation a third party cannot rescue the victim from the original wrong (such as the abusive form of military training or the unsafe work conditions). Consequently one cannot be guilty of *abandoning* the victim to these fairly tangible harms. But silence here can constitute what I call "*moral* abandonment" of a victim whose protests are blocked and whose status as a member of the moral community is thereby degraded. Who could be potentially accountable for such moral abandonment? The most likely are the relatively unthreatened members of the institution who know, or should know, what the situation is. But I do not think it can always be safely restricted to them. There can be circumstances when someone outside of the institution can be legitimately described as morally abandoning a victim and situations where even fairly vulnerable third parties face a moral call to protest.

Because of all that is involved in victim oppression, there are two *victim-focused* motives for third-party protest in addition to the motive of disassociation from moral wrongs or the organization responsible for them. These two motives, I believe, have more moral urgency than the disassociation argument. First, the protester is signalling that the victim should be treated in accordance with the moral status implied by membership in the community. If we are not in a position to ensure that someone is treated fairly, if we cannot, for example, ensure that a victim receives redress for a serious wrong, we can still acknowledge and declare that fairness is owed. It is a declaration of the victim's worth or standing in the protester's eyes, since protesting means that serious injustice to that person matters, even though one is unable to rectify it.

Second and relatedly, it realigns some relevant relationships, especially if one is a member of the same institution as the original wrongdoer, and it places third parties in what I believe to be a morally appropriate relationship with powerless victims. It is an act of *moral solidarity* with the victim, which breaks into the "isolation" mentioned above. It thus helps to amend or forestall moral abandonment, something I am claiming as a moral priority over protecting the sensibilities of the institutional agent(s) responsible for the wrong—and that is meant to include agents who act with a nonculpable lack of awareness.

Protesting also signals to the relevant institutional agent(s) that although one can be counted upon to give a reflective, honest, and whole-some loyalty, this is not to be equated with mindless, irresponsible, and ultimately self-serving acquiescence. This signal, of course, is why it requires a proper amount of moral courage on the part of the protester. This part of realigning the relationships is rather like Hill's point about disassociation, but the emphasis here is on what constitutes morally sound loyalty and how that should be incorporated into various relationships.

FOCUS ON THE FEELINGS OF THE VICTIMS?

Ex hypothesi in the situations considered, the protest will not bring about any of the desirable tangible effects mentioned earlier in the chapter (such as bring redress to the victim, reform in the wrongdoers, and so on). But it might be suggested that the two victim-focused motives are still aimed at tangible effects of a sort, namely, less painful feelings for the victim.

Of course in a utilitarian calculation of effects, the prospective better feelings of the victim would be weighed against (at least) the tension and unease of the protester and the anger or embarrassment of the person hearing the protest. The victim would probably lose. But then, it will be suggested, the two victim-focused motives for protest give a special priority to the feelings of the victim over the feelings of the two other main players. So the motives still aim at a kind of tangible effect, and that is what justifies the third-party protest. It is, therefore, a consequentialist type of justification.

In response to this, I believe the justifiably painful feelings of alert recipients of victim oppression are very important, the more so since they are standardly not perceived by the more fortunate, and if perceived at all, are often misconstrued. Where in practice possible, the victim should know, indeed be consulted, about the protest. Keeping the victim in the dark is but another contribution to the suppressed moral status of the victim, even if such an exclusion makes things more comfortable for the others involved (especially for those agents responsible for the original wrong or the victim oppression). And it is appropriate for the protester to encourage and listen to the victim and to hope that the act of solidarity will bring a little relief to the pain of the situation.

But if none of this is possible, and the victim cannot therefore feel better because of the protest, the two victim-focused motives given earlier remain. I believe it is still important to signal the person's entitlement to appropriate treatment as a member of the moral community even if, regretfully, s/he does not hear of it. And relatedly, I think we can form an appropriate or right relationship with someone even if that person is unaware of it.

Just as we can form an inappropriate relationship the other person is unaware of, so too we can form a basically sound relationship unknown to the person. And surely we do allow for the former. A person can repeatedly betray and pour scorn on a friend's deepest confidences when talking to others, yet the betrayed friend may never know. These acts fundamentally affect the real nature of the relationship. They seriously distort the relationship, so that not only is it not a genuine friendship, also it would be morally inappropriate even between mere acquaintances.

Equally, we can contribute to a morally sound relationship where the other person never knows of it. Both of the victim-focused motives for futile protest in a sense involve contributing to morally appropriate relationships. The protest declares the victim's equal moral standing with other members, which the moral community at large has failed to respect, and it aligns the protester with the victim in an act of moral solidarity. No good tangible consequences may follow. There may not even be any relief to the victim's painful feelings, especially if the victim knows nothing of the protest. In a strange way, given what we owe the victim, it may be morally crucial that the wrongdoer be aware of the protest, while highly desirable but not crucial that the victim be aware. That is to say, the moral call to protest remains even if the victim is not in a position to hear of it, since it nonetheless contributes to the relationship of solidarity with the victim.

Nothing in what I have argued for here challenges the carefully developed points found in Hill's essay, but I think it is significant that in the position he argues for and those he critiques, Hill considers justifications concerning the wrongdoer, the third-party protester, and justice in the abstract, but no justification clearly centered around possible obligations toward the victims. Perhaps it is fair to say that in spite of the relatively recent work on racism, sexism, and exploitative economic systems, the main body of literature within philosophical ethics still incorporates the legacy of ignoring the perspective of the victims, especially those without power, and this seriously hinders our building an adequate conceptual apparatus for examining certain types of moral wrong and associated obligations.

Some of the grounds for protest considered so far in this chapter can of course also be relevent to protesters who are victims, not third parties. Victims may try to prevent those responsible for the wrong from escalating their acquisition and use of power. They may hope to raise society's awareness of a serious but subtle form of wrong, or they may even protest in unfavorable situations in order to form relationships of solidarity with other, perhaps totally silenced, victims. They may also protest as an expression of their moral integrity, and this connects with a particularly poignant ground for victim protest: when their self-respect is under attack, victims may find that protesting helps them to maintain their self-respect, or, if it cannot be maintained, then protest at least indicates a refusal to cooperate with this attack.

This second possibility is one I wish to return to later, in chapter 6. It may seem paradoxical to speak of self-respect being lost even though the person steadfastly refuses to cooperate with the attack, but I will argue that it can indeed happen if the oppression within a person's life situation is extensive. It may even be unavoidable. For the moment, however, I will postpone that discussion.

SELF-COMPLICITY

Nonprotest is an act of compliance with being wronged, and in general such compliance undermines self-respect. Oppression standardly incorporates mechanisms that function to make the victims more and more compliant. Those at the receiving end of some relationship that is morally inappropriate may not be aware of it, perhaps because it involves a mental attitude alone, or perhaps because the recipient has been trained to see the relationship as appropriate or has not critically examined it. Even when the victim is aware, there may be nothing that can be done about it without paying a heavy price. Unprotesting compliance with the unsound relationship can bring with it tangible rewards. Bernard Boxill notes that "oppressors, no doubt, desire to be justified. They want to believe more than that their treatment of others is fitting; they want those they mistreat to condone their mistreatment as proper, and therefore offer inducements and rewards toward that end."[12] The pupil in the authoritarian school and the military recruit with abusive training officers will find their situations far less grim if they comply with the injustices meeted out to them. Indeed, they are likely to be rewarded.

This same pattern is found in the situation of many women. In many places a wife who sees her whole life as an extension of her husband's, and her one goal to further whatever goals he has, will be rewarded with a higher material standard of living than if she tries to make a life for herself in her own right. The failure of a life in her own right is not of course some natural misfortune unfolding, but rather the result of traditions and structures in place that hinder her opportunities and her success and may even penalize any attempt she makes to avoid the unsound, controlled, and overly dependent relationship. She is aware that she will very probably remain unemployed or be employed in a series of temporary, low-paying, physically demanding jobs, and have no means, therefore, to make her long-term life situation fulfilling and secure. If she has children and takes them with her, their future will be similarly bleak. On the other hand, if she complies with the distorted relationship, her standard of living will tend to be higher, both during the earlier portions of her life and even more so in the years when she is elderly.

These losses of tangible goods can be so daunting that sometimes someone stays in a relationship that is more overtly abusive, perhaps even involving physical abuse. But the point here is that even if such abuse is present, there is often a clear and major loss of tangible goods that accompanies noncompliance.

Sometimes the price paid for noncompliance in a morally unsound relationship is even greater. Indeed, it is not unusual for someone to be faced with two options: either to be complicitous in the distorted relationship or to object and suffer retaliatory harm. Sometimes an abused woman may have well-grounded fears for her life and the lives of her children if she tries to leave the relationship. The recruit in the military may find that any attempt to secure fair treatment results in being assigned to abusively demanding chores and exercises.

Whether we speak of the "withdrawal" of the usual, tangible rewards or the more direct inflicting of retaliatory harms, the victim is facing a "lesser of two evils" kind of choice: either comply with the wrongdoing or suffer the penalties directed to the noncompliant. Even if we set aside here outright physical coercion, many societies are still structured in such a way that this "lesser of two evils" kind of choice is all there is for many people, both women and men. The options are bleak, since they may pit minimally decent material conditions and social standing against the refusal to comply with their own denigration. The former are attainable only by choosing to enter into inappropriate relationships, or at least by choosing to stay in them. Either way, achieving decent material conditions means being complicitous in unsound relationships with oneself as victim. So the person faces a double bind, forced to choose between obvious tangible harms and some distorted relationship, the latter, however, often receiving scant if any recognition, let alone sympathy, from others because of its relative lack of visibility compared with the tangible harms.

If someone is repeatedly faced with such a choice at major points in life and repeatedly decides to minimize the tangible harms, the self-complicity in the distorted relationships accumulates. One can make fairly brisk comments about "there being no choice," but in a literal sense this is false. It is part of the genius of civilized oppression that victims—at least those who are adults with normal capacities—are induced to *choose* to enter into inappropriate relationships by being placed under severe prudential constraints. And so long as any element of choice is involved, victims have to live with the humiliating recognition of their own role in entering the distorted relationship. They were heavily constrained, but they were not outright physically coerced, and that distinction is crucial for the likely effects of demoralization to occur.

On the other hand, we can glibly suggest that one should not be self-complicitous in unsound relationships, and this should be good advice. But in the circumstances we are considering, such a steadfast refusal can come at a terrible cost, for example, so far as basic living conditions are concerned. And there is the final irony that in most societies, being in really poor shape with respect to material living conditions means that you are treated with a general lack of respect. So if some oppressive structure is at work, then those made vulnerable by it may find that something essential to maintaining self-respect and integrity makes them the object of disrespect by many. The affluent but totally submissive wife may share in the respect given to her husband, whereas the single mother who, say, decides not to marry someone who is becoming abusive may well remain in poverty and be treated as of no account by many. As a general claim, it is a myth that nearly all people in fact respect those who strive to maintain self-respect. In industrialized societies, at least, respect is often given to public "success" and the power it brings with it.

Being at the receiving end of morally unsound relationships with no recourse justifiably undermines a person's confidence about life. Being in several such relationships is often accompanied by a distortion in the relationship to oneself. It is undermined in all but the strongest of inner selves. But knowingly taking an active role in moving into or staying in such relationships can lead to a particularly devastating collapse of self-respect. Recognized self-complicity, even for serious prudential reasons, threatens the status of "a victim pure and simple," and that in turn leads to both self-doubt about one's personal integrity and often a moral disapproval of the role one played even while feeling all but literally coerced into it. Such unsound relationships, then, are often invisible to bystanders and even contributing agents, even when the victim is aware; they are standardly intractable to remedies within the victims' control (and obviously so in the extreme cases where mental attitude alone is at fault); they often lead to distortions in the victims' relationship to their own self; and, finally, they tend to have the least powerful members of society as recipients. For these reasons they constitute a particularly grim kind of evil.

For the same reasons, protesting serious wrongs against oneself is tied fairly closely to maintaining self-respect in the face of maltreatment (although I will argue in a later chapter that there may come a point when maintaining self-respect literally cannot be done). Bernard Boxill writes that a victim can be "driven to make his claim to self-respect unmistakable. . . . His protest affirms that he has rights. More important, it tells everyone that he believes he has rights."[13] In Western societies there are still some long-standing societal structures and habits that repeatedly subject some vulnerable members to ill treatment and injustice. They function as mechanisms that subordinate and control those members in one or more aspect of their lives. The unrelenting nature of it often wears down the resistance of the victims to the point where they comply with their demeaned status, not only in action but also in mind. They may, for example, start to let go of their belief that they have a particular right if defending that right brings retaliation fairly consistently. The sheer impact of repeated mistreatment may lead some victims to despise their day-to-day lives, perhaps even themselves, and move them to seek better treatment, quite often by ceasing to defend their basic rights.

On the other hand, protest in the face of mistreatment signals the victims' refusal to comply with such manipulations of their intellectual and moral judgment. They know that they have a right to fairer treatment and their protests convey that they have not been intimidated or browbeaten into thinking otherwise. If they cannot secure justice, they nonetheless refuse to surrender their minds. "Freedom of thought" is not especially concerned with a right to think that pink spiders lived on Mars in centuries past. It is more crucially concerned with the exercise of intellectual judgment, as honestly and carefully as one is able, after reflection on evidence and reasons and contrary views, but above all, with no intellectual accommodation being made in response to intimidation, manipulation, or denigration. For those who have been recipients of oppressive relationships and systematic unfairness, freedom of thought may be the most crucial form of resistance. Protest, as an expression of this resistance, can have a sustaining role for their self-respect, even though there is a limit to their individual control over it.

For victims of wrongdoing, trapped in relationships of unequal power, the suppression of their protests is but an indicator of the morally unsound, controlling relationships involved in what I have called victim oppression, relationships that sometimes call for interventions in the form of apparently futile third-party protest.

For the victims, maintaining self-respect is important, but there are limits to their control over self-respect, and in particular there are limits that are not determined by their psychological resources. This is something I will argue for in a later chapter, but that argument must be postponed until we have a fuller account of what membership in the moral community involves.

The next chapter looks further at the situation of those at the receiving end of oppression by examining another frequent component of oppressive situations, the phenomenon of "blaming the victim."

NOTES

1. Bernard R. Boxill, "Self-Respect and Protest," *Philosophy and Public Affairs* 6, no. 4 (Fall 1976): 58–69, 69.

2. In some cases the same basic point applies to the original wrong as well, since it too will turn out to involve an ongoing relationship, not simply a few isolated incidents of tangible harm.

3. Cited in Hannah Arendt, "The Deputy: Guilt by Silence?" in *Amor Mundi,* ed. James W. Bernauer (Dordrecht: Martinus Nijhoff, 1987), 53.

4. Cheshire Calhoun, "Responsibility and Reproach," *Ethics* 99, no. 2 (January 1989): 389–406.

5. Calhoun, 405–6.

6. Arendt, 58.

7. Thomas E. Hill, "Symbolic Protest and Calculated Silence," in his *Autonomy and Self-Respect* (Cambridge: Cambridge University Press, 1991), 56.

8. Hill, 58.

9. Hill, 57.

10. Hill, 63.

11. Hill, 57.

12. Boxill, 65.

13. Boxill, 69.

Chapter 5

Reversing the Charges

In situations of wrongdoing, where protest, blame, and defense often come into play, it becomes important on all sides how the situation is described. In cases of civilized oppression the victims may have to face not only the suppression of protest but also dangerous misdescriptions of the overall situation. In particular, there is a recurring set of phenomena involving misleading attributions of responsibility. They can be grouped together under the familiar phrase "blaming the victim" where this phrase is used in the pejorative sense to indicate that something morally objectionable is involved. But there are a number of different forms and no commonly accessible articulation of them, and this makes the relevant incidents and the moral issues involved hard to spot. So in this chapter I offer a framework for different categories of "blaming the victim" incidents and then explain several common ways in which they can be objectionable. Some of these are inherently difficult to see by nonvictims, and they can occur even when the "blamer" is well intentioned toward the victim. As we will see, such moral oversights are particularly prone to occur in oppressive situations.

A COMMON ELEMENT?

"Blaming the victim," in the pejorative sense I am concerned with, usually involves attributing to the victim of harm some responsibility for it, when in fact the person is not responsible. But some practices commonly called "blaming the victim" do not blame in the literal sense of ascribing moral fault. I will say more about this below, but it immediately raises the question of what, if anything, the cluster of practices called "blaming the victim" have in common. I suggest there are perhaps just three features: first, when the label "blaming the victim" applies, there is harm of some kind to someone, there is a victim; second, the act of blaming the victim focuses on the victim in an inappropriate and typically unflattering way in accounting for the harm; and third, the victim-blaming is in some morally inappropriate way damaging to the victim.

Even without further development, this basic characterization allows for the fact that although in most cases of "blaming the victim" the initial harm is in fact a moral harm (involving a moral wrong), there is at least one kind of case where the harm is nonmoral, that is, not due to some moral wrong. Also, it is compatible with moral harms committed by nonculpable agents, perhaps acting with an excusable lack of awareness. And although many cases involve accusing the victim of some moral fault, the common elements above allow for the fact that some cases do not. Motives are intentionally not mentioned in the basic characterization, since one of the claims I will make is that blaming the victim is surprisingly often motivated by compassion for the victim. Nor is it specified who is doing the blaming. It may be the accountable agent, an onlooker, some more general "voice" like a long-standing tradition or common saying, or the actual victim.

The ways of blaming the victim are diverse. Susan Wendell, for example, mentions four possibilities in her paper, "Oppression and Victimization."[1] But I would like to bring some intelligible order to the range of possibilities, so far as possible, something that will help make the variety of cases more memorable.

A POSSIBLE FRAMEWORK

The first category of blaming the victim mentioned below is atypical in that the actual harm the victim has experienced is nonmoral. In the other categories the victim has in fact been the recipient of some moral harm (harm where some moral wrong is involved), so there is an accountable agent. After the first category, the other five move as systematically as possible through the different degrees of shifting the responsibility away from the actual agent of the harm, from total dismissal of responsibility to partial shifts. So each category refers both to the situation and the claim(s) being made about the victim.

Category 1—There is in fact nonmoral harm, but then the victim is inappropriately "blamed" for it.

We do speak of "victims" of nonmoral harm, "the victims of the hurricane," "victims of the cholera epidemic," and so on. Nonmoral harm includes justified harms, accidents involving no negligence, and also harms of natural origin, like an illness, providing again there is no negligence. The victim may be claimed to be morally at fault, or some false or irrelevant claim about some nonmoral failing of the victim may be given as the reason why the harm occurs. For example, in past decades parents suffering the terrible loss of an infant to "crib death" (now usually called "sudden infant death syndrome"), were often blamed for the death, even though there was no evidence of neglect or any nonmoral failing on their part that would account for the child's death.

Category 2—There is in fact moral harm (harm involving a moral wrong), but then all accountability of the actual agent is dismissed by simply denying there is any harm at all.

Typically this is accompanied by some claim about a moral or nonmoral failing of the victim who makes the "false" claim. Victims protesting the actual harm are "imagining things" or "making false accusations," perhaps hysterically, perhaps maliciously. For example, it is no surprise that a woman typically objects to being called "a broad," as demeaning or prejudicial, while supervisors or investigators regard it as utterly harmless.

A more general kind of example is the response from a significant proportion of people in privileged positions to claims from minorities, women, the physically handicapped, and others about the ongoing bias, contempt, and discrimination directed toward them. With all the overwhelming evidence of how commonplace and habitual such behavior is in Western societies, members of the targeted groups who name the problem still find their credibility routinely attacked and their claims dismissed as "just a matter of personal perception" (meaning here, a subjective projection with no basis in fact). Sometimes these denials amount to a denial of any harm at all, in which case the instances belong in this second category.

Category 3—There is in fact moral harm, but then all moral responsibility of the actual agent is dismissed by the claim that the harm is nonmoral (for example, a natural harm).

As with the previous category, this is typically accompanied by some claim about a moral or nonmoral failing of the victim. A woman in the military objected to sexual harassment by her supervisor. An internal investigation decided there was no such harassment. But since the woman experienced distress and disruption of work in response to the supervisor's comments, it was because the woman was either "oversensitive" or "had a problem with authority figures" (which of course was true; she was having enormous problems with them). In effect, the military was claiming the harm was nonmoral and due to her character defects, something for which the supervisor was not responsible.

The same kind of move is sometimes seen with denials of oppressive harms: that there is harm of some kind is acknowledged (so the cases do not belong in the second category), but the harm arises out of the defects of the "victims." They are again "oversensitive," "paranoid," "thin-skinned," "have no sense of humor," or whatever, that is, usually the "blame" points to some nonmoral defect in the victim.

In Nova Scotia, Canada, a fourteen-year-old hockey player, a Micmac Indian, was subjected to a barrage of taunts from about twenty adult spectators. As I recall the newscast, he was so devastated by them he had to withdraw from the game. So he was harmed by the taunts. But was this a moral harm, specifically, because of racism, or was it the youngster's "problem"? In the words of a Nova Scotia hockey referee, "The only three words I heard were the term 'Indian,' the term 'wagon burner,' and then a noise like an Indian. I don't know how you would classify it as racist."[2] Enough said.

Category 4—There is in fact moral harm, but then it is claimed that in accounting for it, we must look at some crucial contribution from the victim, something involving some moral or nonmoral failing. The victim may be held wholly or partly responsible, but even if the victim and actual agent are both "blamed," the victim's contribution is claimed to be crucial in that without it, no harm would have occurred.

Some of the particular forms in this category are easily recognized. *The victim may be accused of (a) intentionally enticing or provoking the harm; or (b) unintentionally providing temptation or provocation, either through negligence or because of some nonmoral failing or problem, like an excusable ignorance of danger.*

Consider the first form. The poor, for example, have always been blamed for their destitution by many of the affluent. William Ryan's famous book *Blaming the Victim* examines this phenomenon.[3] Also, one can still hear it said of a woman who has been sexually assaulted that "she must have led him on," or something equally insulting, said even by complete strangers who know nothing about the case. For example:

> Rape victim: "The first staff member who saw me was a psychiatrist. His first words were, 'Haven't you really been rushing toward this very thing all your life?' He knew nothing about me, nothing! I had never been to a psychiatrist."[4]

Even child victims are accused, often by their assailants. In cases of incest, they are often accused by family members other than the attacker. Wives have tried to protect their husbands, the attackers, by accusing their children of enticement.

In this category, one of the most sordid cases reported in Canada concerns a weekly newspaper in Vancouver, British Columbia, which carried a half-page statement by a local resident saying that the murder of fourteen female engineering students at Montreal's Ecole Polytechnique in 1989 was a political act to warn that feminism had gone too far. It ended with an apology to the killer Marc Lepine for allowing the women's movement to go unchecked. The implication was clearly that the women in the movement provoked the man into murder and suicide, and that therefore an apology was due. The publisher of the newspaper is reported to have said that he does not print advertisements that he finds offensive to women, such as those for escort agencies, but that he does not believe there is anything wrong with this "ad": "I don't feel that in that ad he's advocating violence against women."[5]

Consider now the particular form that charges "negligence." For example, in a news report of a women mugged while window shopping, a police officer noted sympathetically that her wallet was in an inside pocket, it was midday, and she was on a busy street. But then a security consultant was interviewed and he pointed out that "one must always be watchful for danger in all circumstances and not be distracted by shop windows. We must all do our bit to prevent crime. A distracted person gazing into windows is just all too tempting." The woman, then, failed to take due precautions, and it seems, was held to be negligent. (The consultant seemed to have no qualms about the vision of daily life he was advocating.) To call this a case of providing temptation is to make a moral judgment that paying attention to a shop window at least partially lessens the moral fault of the mugger. If the consultant believes that the attack would not have occurred if the woman had not been "distracted," then that, combined with the unreasonable moral assessment he gives of the situation, would make it a classic case of blaming the victim (via a charge of negligence).

Those cases in this fourth category that lay moral blame on the victim—from form (a) and some from form (b) above—are probably the closest to *classic cases of victim-blaming*. In these cases the victim of the (moral) harm is morally blamed for it via a charge of intentional or negligent wrong, such that the harm would not have happened without this crucial contribution from the victim.

Category 5—There is in fact moral harm and the crucial responsibility of the actual agent is acknowledged (that is, it is acknowledged that the agent would have harmed the victim regardless of any contribution from the latter), but then it is claimed that some contribution from the victim makes the harm more serious than it would otherwise have been, and that that contribution involves some moral or nonmoral fault of the victim.

In more than one sexual assault case in the 1970s, where the woman physically resisted the assault and was then critically injured or killed, a police officer commented sadly, "well, of course, she tried to fight back." Since in several countries then it was standard police advice not to resist an attack, the implication was that the woman was partly responsible for the harm being as dreadful as it was. Sometimes it seemed to be thought of as a moral fault, such as negligence in not having asked about police advice or arrogance in thinking that she "knew better." But more often it was thought of as some nonmoral failing: some personality problem such as panicking in a crisis or—a favorite one—just being "silly": "It was such a silly thing to do." Only recently and only in a few places has it been recognized that both fighting back and not resisting have serious grounds in their favor, given the possible harms involved, and that the decision is the woman's prerogative and to be respected either way.

Category 6—There is some harm, and any responsibility for it by an agent is acknowledged (including responsibility for how serious it is), but once the harm has occurred, then it is claimed that something untoward in the victim's response makes the ultimate outcome worse than it would otherwise have been, and that that response involves some moral or nonmoral fault of the victim.

Again, some particular forms are common. In the first two, the initial harm can be either moral or nonmoral. *The victim may be charged with (a) overreacting to the harm,* perhaps by describing it in exaggerated terms, or by an emotional response out of proportion to the harm, so that the distress is far more than it should be. This response is usually thought of as a nonmoral failing of the victim, although once in a while someone is accused of maliciously giving an exaggerated description of what happened. *Or the victim may be charged with (b) failing to limit or reduce the harm once it has occurred.* This is often accompanied by some claimed character flaw, such as being apathetic, passive, or brooding, placing no value on oneself, giving up too easily, and so on, but may involve a moral charge, such as being "willfully stubborn." *A third common charge that applies when the initial harm was moral harm is that of (c) protesting the harm in an inappropriate manner.* The protest is "too quick," "too angry," or "at the wrong time."

Where there is moral harm and an actual agent, then responses (a) and (c) are claimed to make the situation worse by "antagonizing the agent," "making it difficult to secure redress," or "losing the sympathy of those around." If the pejorative sense of "victim-blaming" applies, these charges and complaints are all inappropriate. Such charges arise repeatedly in oppressive situations of long standing where agents contributing to the oppression (whether consciously or otherwise) are unaccustomed to the oppressed protesting their maltreatment. In fact, any description of the wrongful harm or any emotional response to it can be called "exaggerated," and almost any kind of protest can be deemed "confrontational." These inappropriate charges all serve to keep the victims subservient and under threat, since anything but silence results in serious charges of character defects of one kind or another by people in positions of power.

These six basic categories reflect the *basic forms* that victim-blaming incidents can take. In all six basic categories, if the pejorative sense of "blaming the victim" applies, then the "blame" is inappropriate and morally objectionable. This is true, then, of the cases I am concerned with in this work. But although the basic categories above point to several ways in which victim-blaming can be objectionable, the actual formulations of the categories do not cover all that quite standardly goes wrong, nor is there a one-to-one correlation between each basic category and some one way in which victim-blaming can be objectionable. So having articulated the *basic categories or forms,* I will now mention what I think are the *most common ways in which such incidents can be objectionable.*

WAYS VICTIM-BLAMING CAN BE MORALLY OBJECTIONABLE

(A) The most readily seen way is the laying of moral blame on an innocent victim, whether that be via the charge of negligence or something stronger. This can occur in all the six categories. What I call "the classic cases of victim-blaming," found in Category 4, involve moral blame of an innocent victim.

(B) In addition, some but not all of these cases involve shifting all or some moral accountability away from the actual agent of moral harm (not all, because some cases involve only nonmoral harm to the victim, as in Category 1). Some cases are more subtle than others in that the speaker does not explicitly declare the actual wrongdoer innocent, but instead steadfastly refuses to use any morally reproachful language in connection with the person.

(C) Many cases claim that some nonmoral failing of the victim played a major role in the situation. With the pejorative sense of victim-blaming, these attributions of some character or personality flaw are either irrelevent or, far more often, simply false. Claims about being "hysterical," "weak," "paranoid," "confused," and so on, even though false, bring embarrassment and humiliation. They are doubly painful when raised in response to a victim's trying to explain or protest a wrongful harm, since they function as a form of intimidation and retaliation toward someone already wronged and seeking a just outcome. It is a dangerous logical mistake to assume that if the claim made is about a nonmoral failing or problem of the victim, then there can be nothing morally objectionable in making that claim.

But besides these, there are other less obvious ways in which victim-blaming can involve something morally objectionable. Without trying to give an exhaustive list, I will mention a few that are common and important, although not so easily seen, and then give clarifying examples in the rest of this chapter.

(D) Some cases of victim-blaming involve denying the victim's actual lack of

safe power in the situation. If the victim accepts the account, it is sometimes a cruel illusion. In some kinds of cases (often involving institutions), it also means that actual problems concerning the power distribution or the abuse of power are not acknowledged, let alone addressed. This denial of the actual power relations can leave the victim feeling guilty about not using safe power that in fact s/he did not have. It also works to invalidate the victim's account of what happened, and if that account is accurate, such invalidation can be immobilizing and demoralizing.

(E) *Some cases of victim-blaming present inappropriate or unreasonable restrictions and deprivations as duties the victims should undertake to protect themselves.*

(F) *Some acts of victim-blaming amount to urging victims into morally inappropriate relationships and a degraded moral status within the moral community.*

(G) *Victim-blaming can involve urging the victim on to a path that inappropriately diminishes self-respect.*

WELL-INTENTIONED MOTIVES FOR VICTIM-BLAMING

A lot of victim-blaming arises out of motives that are morally reprehensible, and we notice these cases first. Some agent or institution may try to deflect accountability for some serious wrong and preserve the desired public image by blaming the victim. Many such cases occur when the victim protests the original harm. And when the victim is claimed to be morally to blame, then any call for redress is rejected. Also, victim-blaming can be motivated by sheer hostility and anger toward the victims, or by the desire to silence victim protest by this form of retaliation, or by a more general desire to keep the victims insecure and subordinate.

But surprisingly often the motive is not so dismal. In fact the main claim I am making about motives for victim-blaming is that they often involve genuine concern for the victim. That is, the pejorative sense of "blaming the victim" is not necessarily excluded just because the motives are good.

In any of the six basic categories, good or bad motives may be at work. No category is restricted to ill-intentioned cases, not even when the victim is outright morally blamed, and not even when the harm is denied altogether. A misguided friend may try, in all sincerity, to convince both herself and her friend (a victim of some harm) that there really is no harm, even to the extent of trying to convince him that he doesn't really feel badly. She so wants him to feel better. Each category can contain both well- and ill-motivated incidents, and quite often the same overt act of blaming the victim can arise from a good or a bad motive.

To say that the pejorative sense of "victim-blaming" can apply in cases where the motive is good is to say that there can be something morally wrong going on even with a good motive. I listed above seven common ways in which something objectionable can be involved (see [A]–[G] on pp. 85–86). Each of the seven ways can be found in cases that are well motivated. The combination that results in most of the moral oversights occurs when the motive is good, and the objectionable nature of what's happening is one of the harder types to spot (like type [E]).

It remains, then, to show how good motives can be associated with morally objectionable incidents and, along the way, offer clarifying examples of the different ways in which a case can be objectionable.

When a victim is wrongfully harmed, then it is morally appropriate for the *harm to be undone, the agent called to account,* and *the victim not to be similarly harmed again.* If the victim has readily available what is needed to achieve these goals, then while we feel sympathy, there is also relief that the victim can take effective action. On the other hand, compassionate and perceptive onlookers are more troubled when the victim seems to lack what is needed to secure these goals.

Also, if you are concerned about the victim, it is quite natural to want to alleviate the person's suffering and distress. And you want your efforts in this regard to be effective, to bear results. It is consequently easy to be victim-focused in ways that leave out of the picture other people who are relevant to the situation. The focus, after all, is on the victim's problem or distress.

SYMPATHETIC GOALS AND INCLINATIONS

These natural inclinations of a sympathetic onlooker, when combined with the three goals mentioned in the earlier paragraph, easily prompt a well-intentioned instance of blaming the victim that is morally objectionable.

Consider the desire that the victim not be subjected to the same kind of harm in the future. This well-intentioned goal can lead us to retell the moral story in such a way that the victim could have prevented the present harm and so can also prevent it in the future. The victim contributed in some way to the present situation, but need not do the same in future. At the very least, the victim may be described as having a lack of power which is strictly "internal" to the person (such as, some character defect), something that can therefore be tackled. We want the victim to have the power to prevent further such harms, and this compassionate wish easily leads to cases that are objectionable in ways (D) or (E).

The window shopper who was mugged and robbed was blamed by the security consultant for looking in the shop window. Supposing he was genuinely concerned to prevent the woman from being similarly harmed in the future, then the implication is that if she always keeps an eye on who is around her, she will be able to prevent a repeat experience. But this is anything but obvious. She may still have to walk down the street if she cannot afford a car or taxi, if the bus stop is at the end of the street, or the route is for pedestrians only, and if that is where the shops and services she needs are located. Even if she looks in no shop windows, there can be enough people on the street to make it impossible not to come within several feet of some of them, no matter how she adjusts her path. If the attack is sudden and vicious, then in practice she may not be able to prevent it. In such a case, blaming her for looking in the shop window—as though not doing so would have prevented the harm—is to deny her actual lack of safe power in such situations, which is objectionable in way (D). It is also objectionable in way (E), since it urges the victim to accept as a duty never looking in a shop window if anyone is within, say, twenty feet, and most of us would consider this an inappropriate restriction. It is a restriction she is free to take on, but the very idea that she "must" or "should" always do this is unreasonable.

A more stunning example of the latter move is mentioned in Susan Brison's paper, "Surviving Sexual Violence," where she points out that "some [Ivy League colleges] have . . . seriously proposed enacting after-dark curfews for women, in spite of the fact that men are the perpetrators of the [sexual] assaults."[6] The line of thinking seems to be that women, for their own protection, ought to have the good sense not to be out after dark, so the colleges have a right to enforce that behavior. Brison points out "how natural it seems to many people to address the problem of sexual violence by curtailing women's lives."[7] It is not the place of the victims to have debilitating restrictions and deprivations imposed upon them. They may choose to restrict themselves (although it is clearly morally outrageous if this is seen by society in general as a proper solution to their being attacked), but they have no moral duty to go to excessive lengths in self-protection, lengths that seriously distort their proper day-to-day lives.

The well-intentioned motive of ascribing future power to the victim by "blaming" the victim now may involve attributing some nonmoral fault to the victim or may involve outright moral blame. Although the compassionate third party will usually refrain from charging intentional enticement or provocation, the victim may be described as (culpably) negligent about the protection of self or possessions. "He ought to 'know better' than to leave his basement door open while working in the back garden." But whether the problem is described in nonmoral or moral terms, in either case it is internal to the victim, so s/he can work on it and hopefully avoid the same contribution to similar situations in the future. This, in turn, should make the person's future safer, which is the ultimate goal here.

Not only onlookers but also the victim may think along these lines, as confirmed in Brison's paper about being sexually assaulted. She writes:

> I wished I could blame myself for what had happened so that I would feel less vulnerable, more in control of my life. Those who haven't been sexually violated may have difficulty understanding why women who survive assault often blame themselves. . . . They don't know that it can be less painful to believe that you did something blameworthy than it is to think that you live in a world where you can be attacked at any time, in any place, simply because you are a woman.[8]

It is significant, then, that even something as morally disturbing as laying outright moral blame on an innocent victim can be motivated by genuine concern for the victim. And trying to see the victim as having the power to prevent the harm in the future (by blaming the victim for some apparently crucial and avoidable contribution this time) is a possible motive in a number of the six categories, even the first. In all such cases the victim-blaming can be objectionable in several ways, including (D).

Consider also the two other frequent desires that are sympathetically disposed toward the victim, namely, wishing the harm to be undone and the agent called to account. Sometimes these goals are materially impossible. Someone paralyzed by a drunk driver cannot have the harm undone, and the agent of a murder–suicide cannot be called to account. But where there is no such impossibility, then situations where the victim cannot secure these two goals (at least, not without being further harmed in a serious way) are often oppressive situations where the victim and the agent of the wrongful harm have very different levels and kinds of power, especially external, socially constructed power. The victim may be facing a corrupt use of institutional or government power, for example. A temptation in such situations is to explicitly or unconsciously deny the lack of safe power on the part of the victim and so blame the victim for the lack of redress. At the very least a bystander may deny the real lack of external power by locating all the problems within the victim, which may seem to make them more approachable by the victim. Paradoxically, the more we care about the victim, the suffering, and the injustice, the more tempting this is, since the motive is to see the victim more in control of securing justice when wrongfully harmed. But all such temptation can lead us to cases that are, again, objectionable in way (D).

Consider Peter, an excellent engineer with first-rate qualifications, who applies for positions for which he is ideally qualified but finds that institutional agents—personnel managers of the various businesses—repeatedly discriminate against him because of his ethnic origin or his age. If this denial of fair opportunity means that he is unemployed or involuntarily part-time employed for a long time, well-meaning and compassionate onlookers see the serious tangible harms of loss of income, and lack of an adequate home and of any social life requiring money. Peter is very likely to receive repeated suggestions that he should give up on that career and look for some other source of income, perhaps teaching engineering in a vocational school, perhaps something other than engineering altogether. If Peter does not follow the well-meant advice, he may well be "blamed" for failing to limit or reduce the harm once it has occurred (Category 6 above). He may be held to be lacking in some nonmoral way (like being too apathetic to seek alternative employment), or he may be held morally culpable via negligence or some moral defect (like being "willfully stubborn").

So what is going wrong here? If Peter follows the well-meant advice and finds an income via other employment, this typically means something for which his qualifications are no longer exceptional, and where there is not the same burning commitment and interest. And given that he is a member of a group frequently discriminated against, say, older applicants, his taking such employment would not in practice be a temporary change. When those doing the hiring are systematically blocking certain groups of applicants, even unconsciously, then if those applicants take other employment, it is standardly greeted—with great relief—as proof that they belong elsewhere. This is one of the major distinctions between those the personnel managers are genuinely prepared to hire but cannot (perhaps because of a budget cut-back), and those who are subject to discrimination and bias. Peter may obtain an alternative income, providing there is no serious economic recession—but at a terrible price. First, there is the loss of the career and the deep fulfillment that comes with being placed where one rightly belongs. An alternative income cannot compensate for this crucial kind of thriving.

But second, there is the harm involved in cooperating with serious injustice toward oneself, because what is really happening here is that a victim of discrimination is being counseled to accomodate himself to being repeatedly treated unjustly. In fact, the structure of the situation is such that he can escape the tangible harms (like poverty) only by acquiescing in serious and protracted injustice to himself. He must stop holding out for a just outcome. It is worth remembering that although all oppression in the widest sense of the word "controls" its victims, still, the specific contexts of oppression differ greatly in that some are geared to trapping the victim in some place or relationship, whereas others are geared to excluding the victim. Wife battering functions to keep the victim in the situation. Employment discrimination functions to exclude the victim from appropriately fulfilling roles. The targeted victims are supposed to find another life path. But to accommodate oneself to repeated and systematic injustice is rather different from adjusting to one manageable and isolated piece of injustice, or from radically adjusting one's life because of chaos brought about by some natural disaster like an earthquake. Different matters are involved.

It is part of the sinister nature of what I call civilized oppression that its victims are placed under severe prudential pressures to acquiesce in serious and ongoing injustice toward themselves. Since this standardly involves giving up some of their most basic moral rights, they are, in effect, under pressure to accept a kind of third-rate membership in the moral community at large. This, in turn, means that the relationships between the victim and other relevant members of the moral community are badly distorted, but the oppressed victim typically has no effective power with which to amend them. If these morally inappropriate relationships are not accompanied by obvious tangible harms, they are often not perceived by nonvictims. And in cases like the one being looked at, if the victim follows the well-intentioned advice and finds some other kind of employment, then the most obvious tangible harms disappear. The distorted relationships and the degraded moral status of the victim within the moral community, however, remain, and urging a victim into them is a common way in which well-motivated instances of victim-blaming can be morally objectionable, that is, way (F).

Furthermore, as we noted in the last chapter, being complicitous in unjustified harm to oneself can undermine a person's self-respect. Of course, not being complicitous in cases like the one being looked at means remaining unemployed, and involuntary poverty also tends to diminish self-respect. But the point is that while there is a small chance of the harm to self-respect being noted when it is associated with poverty, there is virtually no chance of its being noted by people in general when it accompanies the taking of new employment. Yet it is the taking of new but totally inappropriate employment that reflects the victim's manipulated complicity in serious injustice toward him/herself. Urging someone on to a path that standardly diminishes appropriate self-respect is another common way in which well-motivated victim-blaming can be morally objectionable, that is, way (G). This remains true even if the alternative course of action (here, staying unemployed) has the same impact. In fact in Peter's situation, it is important to realize that both the main options are objectionable. Oppressive structures commonly control their victims via double binds, and although they may be perceived in the classic case where both options involve obvious tangible harms, they are hardly ever seen by nonvictims when one option is harmful in some other serious but less tangible kind of way. A great deal of unfairness in describing the situation, and a great deal of unintended harm and pain can occur when sympathetic bystanders see only half of what is involved.

THE LIMITATIONS OF ONLOOKERS

Given Peter's situation, these missed perceptions by uninitiated but sympathetic bystanders are understandable. A victim who resists being complicitous in serious injustice toward him/herself where such resistance leaves the victim with ongoing tangible harms often strikes us, as onlookers, as passive, as someone who in fact lacks the ability to act or to resist oppression. It is the tangible harms that naturally draw our attention as onlookers, and when we see no apparent resistance to them, then we often see no resistance at all, something for which the victim is "blamed" in one way or another.

If as bystanders we do come to reflect on the elusive but crucial relationships and personal moral status here, then we may still return to our original advice, especially if our own situation has always been far more fortunate than the victim's. We want to alleviate the victim's suffering, but if we lack first-hand experience of both kinds of pain, then the suffering caused by poverty or unemployment is still much easier to come to understand than the pain of being urged, expected, or manipulated into cooperating in major and relentless injustice toward oneself.

And if we ever begin to come to grips with that second kind of pain, we may even then repeat the same advice. After all, we want to be effective, to make a difference, and if the power relations that unjustly control the victim cannot be altered in the foreseeable future, then we may again urge the victim to focus on the more tangible harms that perhaps can be lessened. But I hope I have said enough to show that when an alert victim is forced to choose between, on the one hand, being stuck with tangible harms, and, on the other hand, being complicitous in cumulative injustice toward oneself and the distorted relationships this involves, the victim need not be confused or passive if the priority is on resisting the latter. Given that both options are morally objectionable, where the priority lies will be an expression of the person's ranking of values. There are serious grounds in favor of either decision, so either one, taken reflectively, deserves respect. If the structure of the situation is not seen, then unless the victim focuses on lessening the more tangible harms, victim-blaming by the more fortunate is predictable. As Marilyn Frye notes in *The Politics of Reality*, "one of the most characteristic and ubiquitous features of the world as experienced by oppressed people is the double bind—situations in which options are reduced to a very few and all of them expose one to penalty, censure or deprivation."[9]

A RECENT DISTINCTION

The main point about the well-intentioned motives sometimes involved in victim-blaming does not strike everyone as obvious. In a fairly recent paper, "Explaining without Blaming the Victim," Patricia Illingworth focuses on one type of victim-blaming, where "victims are held to be morally responsible for the harm that they have experienced."[10] (These cases seem to match the subset in my Category 4, referred to as "classic cases" of victim-blaming.) Illingworth then explains a distinction between what she calls "blame-the-victim arguments" and "free-the-victim statements." The former attempt to "shift moral responsibility" onto the victim.[11] It is clear that they are held to be morally objectionable. As an example, she points out that sexually assaulted women are sometimes blamed for "provocative clothing" or "a friendly glance" that allegedly "encouraged" the attack.[12]

Free-the-victim statements, on the other hand, "identify the behavior characteristics of victims for the purpose of enabling the victim, either directly or indirectly, to deflect further victimization."[13] They are characterized in terms of this good intention. From Illingworth's writing, it seems clear that they are not thought of as morally objectionable. One example of such a statement describes characteristics of "high-risk" patients with respect to "prohibited sexual relations" between therapists and patients, and a second example identifes nine characteristics of children that "make them vulnerable to sexual abuse."[14] Finally, Illingworth claims that "the most important distinction between [blame-the-victim arguments and free-the-victim statements] is that the former are prescriptive whereas the latter are descriptive."[15] This is not so easy to be clear about, but I think it means that the former lay moral blame on the victim, whereas the latter describe features or behavior of the victim. She writes that "Although founded on good intentions, there is a tendency by some people to conflate free-the-victim statements with the blame-the-victim argument."[16]

Illingworth gives an incisive analysis of the issues involved in patient–therapist sex, locating several false assumptions that are likely to lead to victim-blaming. For example, an observer may assume the patient's "seductive behaviour" is completely voluntary when it is not (which is especially likely if the patient has been the victim of child sexual abuse). But when we move to the general account of what is and is not morally objectionable in victim-blaming situations, Illingworth and I seem to differ.

We share some common ground: we both hold that shifting moral blame onto an innocent victim is clearly objectionable. (Although usually hostilely motivated, I mentioned earlier that even something this objectionable need not be. Well-meaning friends of the victim, even victims themselves, sometimes do it, often without recognizing the fact.) Where we part company is on free-the-victim statements.

First, Illingworth's work reads as though any utterance that fits into one of her two types of statements fits into just one of them. References to "the friendly glance" or "the provocative clothing" of a sex-assault victim, for example, are mentioned only as examples of blame-the-victim statements. But in fact even the "provocative clothing" claim can stem from the good intention characterizing the free-the-victim statements: "Ms. X. unfortunately did not seem to realize that her clothing was provocative and made her vulnerable to attack." Rarely if ever does the *substance* of a sincere utterance guarantee the speaker's motive here. But it may well be that on this point, Illingworth is just not making explicit something I think deserves to be.

My second claim is, therefore, the more important, namely, that the good intention that characterizes free-the-victim statements together with the statement's being descriptive does not ensure the moral soundness of the act. If Illingworth is using the term "descriptive" to imply that moral blame is not being attributed to the victim, then, by definition, that is one type of moral wrong that is excluded here. But to assume that the act is therefore morally innocuous would be to make the mistake of assuming that nothing else can be going morally wrong with the act.

Of course, if something can be objectionable about making a free-the-victim statement, then Illingworth might call it something other than "victim-blaming." Her focus, after all, is on just one type of victim-blaming, whereas I am dealing with more than that one category. But this would be a terminological difference. The substantive question lies in whether the characterization of free-the-victim statements is sufficient to preclude anything morally objectionable going on (regardless of how we would label any such objectionable matter). If our answers to this differ, then we hold positions that differ in a morally substantive way.

Since free-the-victim claims are by definition descriptive (and well motivated), they do not explicitly assign moral blame to the victim. But the crucial question is whether something can still be going morally wrong, something other than assigning moral blame to the victim. That is to say, could the use of a free-the-victim claim constitute a "victim-blaming incident" as I have analyzed the phrase? Could the incident be objectionable in any of ways (B)–(G), for example?

Claims function differently in ordinary conversations from the way they do in formal logic exercises. We need to understand not only the logical implications of the claim itself but also what is implied, often tacitly, by how the claim is used. Such things as where the claim is embedded in a conversation, what intonations are used, what the overall situation is, all affect the implications of the utterance. These implications are not logically guaranteed, but they are reasonably justified, and they are vital to negotiating daily life. Even conversational acts of omission often take on moral significance in a given situation. Although Illingworth defines a "free-the-victim statement" as one that is intended to "enable the victim to deflect further victimization" and that does not ascribe moral blame to the victim, it is still possible for things to go morally wrong in at least ways (B), (C), and (E).

Suppose I am the campus residence supervisor and white, and that three men from the residence, all black, have been attacked just outside the building and found badly beaten, with racist hate words scrawled on the ground. In an important meeting I am asked what I think of it all and my only response is: "You know, their being out 'til dark, and each one alone like that, it makes them very vulnerable, and we none of us want students to be hurt." There is a long silence, but that is all I have to say. My refusal to express any moral outrage or to lay any moral blame on the perpetrators would, I think, rightly be found highly objectionable by anyone deeply concerned about racism, and especially so by the black community on campus. My only response to the incident is victim focused and refers to the victims' apparently dangerous behavior. I do not denounce their attackers, I do not blame them—but I should. Such acts of omission are failures to be in moral solidarity with the victims of a clear moral wrong, failures to endorse their justified outrage, and this can be especially reprehensible if the victims are members of some group having a very rough time trying to be treated with moral respect and equality in our society. The incident becomes objectionable in part because of what I refuse to say. I could also very reasonably be taken to be suggesting that such "vulnerable" students should not be out after dark, and especially not alone. They should avoid such danger. My response, I think, is objectionable, in ways (B) and (E). Readers can probably think of other examples.

CUMULATIVE OPPRESSION AND EMOTIONAL RESPONSES

Everyone may be on the receiving end of a blaming-the-victim incident at some time, but victims of oppression are on the receiving end repeatedly. Oppression involves the systematic misuse of power over the less powerful. The various groups of victims tend not to have the same robust public standing as the agents responsible. They do not have the same public "voice," they are not heard publicly as often, and they are not accorded the same credibility as the favored, more powerful group(s). Consequently they have a very difficult time alerting the powerful and privileged to the ongoing and systematic oppressive harms, since the listeners, by their very social situation, do not experience them. The full dimensions of the harm, especially the serious but less tangible aspects (like badly distorted relationships, or attacks on self-respect) are often not seen by nonvictims. The full significance and impact of repeated harms are not grasped by many whose lives are free of such accumulations. The various ways in which a person can be without safe power are not visible to those with more power than they have any awareness of. For these reasons and more, accounts from articulate and accurate victims are often dismissed as "exaggerated" or even "without foundation." If the people claiming to be victims actually are harmed where, in seemingly parallel situations, members of the favored and powerful group are not, then clearly it must be "their problem" somehow. This response is doubly strong where the oppression is civilized, since it is harder to spot power at work when it does not involve outright physical force or the use of law, and it is far harder to spot one's own involvement in such oppression, most especially when the involvement is habitual, expected, and perhaps completely unconscious. It is no accident that so many of the examples of blaming-the-victim incidents involve members of standardly oppressed groups.

We have already noted that socially privileged bystanders and agents often do not grasp the components of civilized oppression. In particular, the serious but less tangible kinds of things that go wrong are not well perceived: the demeaning humor, the degraded public self, the inadequate support power, the abuse of interactive power, the refusal to engage, the quiet suppression of protest, the moral abandonment, and so on. When some incident involving such a matter occurs, a victim who displays indignation, dismay, or anger may be accused of "being overemotional" or "having no sense of proportion." There is little or no awareness of what the incident involves, so in the absence of obvious material harm, the victim's emotions are condemned. This is a Category 3 type of victim-blaming, already illustrated earlier in the chapter: there is moral harm, but the agent's moral responsibility is dismissed by the claim that the harm is nonmoral (that is, a natural harm). If the person is harmed by the incident, if it causes a significant amount of distress, then it is because of an oversensitivity problem, since there was nothing at all untoward in the incident. The whole thing is a result of the individual's defect of character.

But even if the elements of the incident, the moral harm, and the agent's responsibility *are* recognized, oppressed victims are especially vulnerable to the type of victim-blaming described in Category 6. More specifically, because of the *cumulative* nature of the harm they experience, they are prone to be charged with making the final outcome worse by overreacting to the harm. This is the final point I wish to explain in this chapter.

In the last few decades, literature dealing with cumulative harm has usually focused on harm to the general or public good. For example, when utilitarianism comes under discussion, questions arise about the kinds of acts the general performance of which will result in harm to the public good. As David Lyons asks, does the wrongness of such acts depend on enough people actually doing the act, or is it enough that a cumulative harm would result if enough people did it?[17] There has been considerable literature on the harm to the public good if, say, many people refrain from voting, and we have all stayed awake nights worrying about the cumulative harm to trampled lawns, but strangely, there has not been the same interest in issues concerning cumulative harm to an individual, not until the more recent work on oppression and institutional functioning.

Oppression by its very nature is not randomly directed. Members of certain groups are routinely targeted; the victims are repeatedly and systematically at the receiving end of the various wrongs and harms involved. As the incidents accumulate, victims may justifiably feel that bit more indignant, more dismayed, or more angry when some all-too-familiar type of degrading situation or incident occurs yet again.

These emotions are assessed by onlookers and even by the agents of whatever happened, and fully justified emotion responses will tend to draw scorn and disapproval. In a paper on forgiveness, Howard McGary points out that emotions "tell us a great deal about our moral characters."[18] It is a matter that naturally arises when discussing forgiveness, at least when that concept is construed as the letting go of feelings of resentment. Norvin Richards, working on the same topic, claims that "to forgive someone for something is to abandon all the hard feelings one bases on this particular episode,"[19] and then writes that failures to forgive may display character flaws, since the "presence [of the hard feelings], and their precise tendency to continue, is itself an expression of one's character. It is because of the sort of person you are that you *this* angry with me for having done *that* to you."[20] Well, not necessarily. It may also depend on how many other people have done that same thing to that same person.

In fairness, Richards is only making explicit the usual assumption that "the particular episode" is the basis for assessing the victim's emotions when wronged. This may cause no problems in cases of isolated acts of wrongdoing, but not so in the case of oppressive harms. The victim is entitled to express the justifiable anger of one who has been repeatedly wronged and who is on the receiving end once more. Whether this is described most appropriately as an emotion response to the incident rather than to the agent is not terribly important for our purposes here. The point is that the victim should not have to suppress the naturally greater dismay or indignation felt at yet another in a long series of demeaning events. That greater emotion is not "an overreaction" nor any other failing of the victim's.[21]

The risk, then, of blaming the victim for "responding inappropriately" to civilized oppression is high for at least the two reasons mentioned: perhaps none of the moral harm involved in the incident is acknowledged given the subtle forms it takes, or even if it is acknowledged, the victim's emotion response may be condemned as excessive if the cumulative nature of the oppressive harm is not recognized. In either case not only is the victim-blaming morally inappropriate, it also functions to suppress fully justified emotion responses, especially if the "blamers" have more power and social status than the victim. It is a fact of life, at least in Western societies, that the less powerful are expected to adjust and control their emotions out of consideration for the "socially more important" persons around them. And of course in the face of outright scorn or disapproval from the more powerful, there are more pressing prudential reasons for complying with this expectation.

For these reasons we can now add to the earlier list one more way in which victim-blaming can be morally objectionable:

(H) *Certain forms of victim-blaming pressure the victims into suppressing their fully justified emotion responses to oppressive incidents.* This imposes upon them a burdensome and unreasonable level of affective self-denial, and when victim-blaming functions in this way, it is but another form of morally inappropriate control of the less powerful who are already victimized. It is therefore another form of what in chapter 4 of this volume I called "victim oppression": it is a way of controlling the already victimized, just like the suppression of protest about the fact that some original protest was blocked.

THE NEED FOR MORAL THEORY

In the work to this point we have examined what actually happens in civilized oppression, and we have sometimes created the conceptual apparatus needed to analyze the mechanisms of civilized oppression by which the victimization of individuals is both maintained and concealed. We have articulated the kinds of wrongs and harms involved, the distortions of relationships, and the forms of control, and we have explored the complex anatomy of underlying power relations and the unobtrusive ways in which they shape the visible surface of social life. It is time to ask if the moral insights gradually accumulating along the way can be given some more unified account. We find in the next chapter that a surprisingly basic component of moral theory lies at the heart of civilized oppression.

NOTES

1. Susan Wendell, "Oppression and Victimization: Choice and Responsibility," *Hypatia* 5, no. 3 (Fall 1990): 15–46, 20.
2. Reported in *Vancouver Sun* [Canadian newspaper], 20 February 1993, A4.
3. William Ryan, *Blaming the Victim*, rev. ed. (New York: Vintage Books, 1976).
4. Diana E. H. Russell, *The Politics of Rape* (New York: Stein & Day, 1975), quoted in her later book, *Sexual Exploitation* (Beverly Hills, Calif.: Sage Publications, 1984), 164. For a revealing summary of "victim-precipitation theories" of rape found in psychological studies, see *Sexual Exploitation*, 164–66.
5. Reported in *Vancouver Sun* [Canadian newspaper], 5 December 1992, B3.
6. Susan J. Brison, "Surviving Sexual Violence," *Journal of Social Philosophy* 24, no. 1 (Spring 1993): 5–22, 18.
7. Brison, 18.
8. Brison, 33.
9. Marilyn Frye, *The Politics of Reality* (Freedom, Calif.: The Crossing Press, 1983), 2.
10. Patricia M. L. Illingworth, "Explaining without Blaming the Victim," *Journal of Social Philosophy* 21, no. 2–3 (Fall/Winter 1990): 117–26, 117.
11. Illingworth, 117.
12. Illingworth, 117–18.
13. Illingworth, 117.
14. Illingworth, 122–23.
15. Illingworth, 123.
16. Illingworth, 117.
17. David Lyons, *Forms and Limits of Utilitarianism* (London: Oxford University Press, 1965), e.g., ix, 2.
18. Howard McGary, "Forgiveness," *American Philosophical Quarterly* 26, no. 4 (October 1989): 343–51, 343.
19. Norvin Richards, "Forgiveness," *Ethics* 99, no. 1 (October 1988): 77–97, 80.
20. Richards, 80–81.
21. For an interesting discussion of the relations between resentment and self-respect see chapter 6, "Character and Society," of Laurence Thomas's *Living Morally* (Philadelphia: Temple University Press, 1989).

Chapter 6

Matters of Principle

The existence of civilized oppression draws us to the underlying, unacceptable moral relationships, and to the self-protecting mechanisms by which they become invisible. The tangible harms inflicted by more blatant oppression elicit obvious moral response. But for the moral appraisal of oppressive relationships we must attend to the nature of the moral community. That will prove to be the source of a more unified account of what is going wrong.

SOME BASIC MORAL RIGHTS AND OBLIGATIONS

The moral community includes moral agents and moral patients: roughly, those capable of being under moral obligation, and those to whom obligations can be owed. Those who are moral patients only would require special consideration, not only in practice, but also in moral theory. But this is far too large and important a project to slip into the present work. For the present purpose the focus is on paradigm members of the moral community, those who are full moral agents as well as patients. Agents of oppression must be in this group. Also, these members, as individuals, have the usual agent capacities, like the ability to think, remember, imagine, and foresee consequences, and so they may appear deceptively well equipped to deal successfully with nonphysical abuses of power. It is, then, within this group that moral subordination is the hardest to spot, and for that reason it is of prime importance to our examination. To prevent cumbersome phrasing in the remaining work, full agent members of the moral community will be referred to simply as "members" from now on.

There are some prima facie rights and obligations associated with the *moral life*, or, if I do a bit of unpacking, they are rights and obligations that arise out of a *life of moral endeavor* undertaken as a *member of the moral community.* The moral life in this sense involves moral inquiry, fallibility, moral fault, accountability, amendment, forgiveness, and so on, and since the rights and obligations concern such features of the moral life, they are especially basic. So people with different substantive moral theories and fundamental moral principles, with resulting differences in more specific moral conclusions, may still agree about them. In this chapter I will look at the most central aspects of the moral life and the rights and obligations associated with them.

Since moral persons can be victims of wrongs as well as agents, and since a serious wrong is by definition something that should never have been, this grounds the right to *protest and call for the amendment* of such wrongs. The word "protest" here covers the full range of relevant actions, from raising a concern to voicing a major objection. Not just the victim of the wrong but all members of the moral community have a right to be concerned about a serious wrong. There is correspondingly a shared right of communication, to bear witness, remonstrate, and intervene in the case of serious wrongs. In fact, I argued in chapter 4 that sometimes a right to protest may become a prima facie obligation to protest, even as a "bystander," if the victim is oppressed.

Also, since moral agents combine the capacity for doing wrongful harm with the capacities for reflection and inquiry, they have an ongoing obligation to *review, revise, and try to extend their moral understanding,* and a right to expect such an ongoing reflective approach in fellow members. Reflection and inquiry cannot ensure sound insights, but without them, oversights and confusions remain undetected and dangerous over-simplifications are never modified. Obligations to consider, to hear, to pay attention, and to inquire correlate with the right of agents to *present to one another information and arguments expected to help* in our moral inquiry, especially when the presenters have first-hand experience of relevant situations or moral phenomena.

Agents are accountable for their actions, and this grounds an obligation to be reasonably willing to explain the reasons for specific decisions that affect others, especially when exercising power over less powerful people who cannot prevent or undo the decision's impact. Those who are both *vulnerable and at the receiving end* of those power-backed decisions have the right to *hear the justification* for those that significantly affect them. This position of course runs counter to much of actual practice where many fairly powerful agents consider that only those with yet more power, specifically power over *them,* have a right to their justifications. They practice what I call an "upward only" accountability.

Even if there are sound reasons why the more powerful agents are making the decision, still, the more vulnerable, affected fellow members of the moral community have the right to *assess those decisions and justifi-*

cations and the right to protest them. Indeed, the fact that they are not in a position to make the decisions themselves means there is all the more reason for these rights to be assured. Their lack of practical power does not justify robbing them of the exercise of their moral judgment in matters so close to them. The right to moral assessment, I argue, is a right of all members of the moral community. It is an intellectual component of moral autonomy, and in the kind of situation described it constitutes most of what is left of their autonomy with respect to what could be life-affecting decisions. For these reasons, the more powerful the agents making the decisions, the more that evasiveness on their part becomes morally dubious.

The last few items combine to suggest that a degree of openness—some willingness to discuss moral issues and explain the reasons for one's moral positions and decisions—is appropriate in a moral community.

I think membership in the moral community grounds a few other rights and obligations, and contrary to increasingly popular assumptions in society at large, even very vulnerable parties can have obligations. For example, if—and I emphasize, "if"—those in a position of some power have made an effort to build the appropriate relationships and have ensured that they are not inaccessible, that contact can be initiated by the less powerful when appropriate, then at that point, I argue, if such a person does seem to do something that raises a concern we have a prima facie obligation to take that concern *to that person first*. This is not a matter of "courtesy," but rather something we owe to a fellow member of the community, someone who has the right to explain anything relevant, clear away any misunderstandings, and possibly offer to amend the situation if indeed the concern is legitimate. Mutual support of this kind between fellow members is a recognition of ordinary moral fallibility, the kind of nonperfection that need not have any significant impact on a person's good moral character. It is a kind of mutual support that both the powerful and, in certain conditions, the less powerful can and should offer. This is contrary to a disturbingly growing trend where victims with relatively less power are actively encouraged, in all circumstances, to keep their concerns from the person in question and instead go, in the first instance, to someone else, often someone "above" the person in some hierarchical organization. It is usually more comfortable for the victim of course, but those with power are still fellow members, and when they are both well intentioned and have taken active measures to help construct appropriate relationships, then we owe them the first hearing of any significant concern.

I have also argued elsewhere that under certain conditions, a victim can have an obligation to *forgive a wrongdoer and support his/her fresh start*,[1] whether the wrongdoer is less or more powerful than the victim. But the items above are probably the most central to the inquiry, struggles, mistakes, reflection, insights, and interactions that constitute the moral life.

These rights and obligations give considerable structure to basic *moral relations*. For example, without agreeing on everything that constitutes a serious moral wrong, it still follows that relationships where the more powerful routinely block meaningful protest of any kind from the more vulnerable are violations of the appropriate moral relations. So too are power relations that routinely block information and arguments from the more vulnerable. This is especially pernicious where the input is on first-hand experience only the less powerful have. Also, when the more powerful make decisions that significantly affect the more vulnerable and yet refuse to give any justification for their decisions, the basic moral relationships are again distorted.

DE FACTO MORAL STATUS

These basic rights and obligations are vital to the moral status of members of the moral community. But at this point we need to introduce an important distinction between what I will call a person's *proper moral status* and a person's *de facto moral status*. The two may differ a great deal. An individual's proper moral status is the status the person morally should have, but his/her actual moral status may be either more or less than it should be. That is to say, an individual's de facto moral status may include more or less than the proper moral status.

I will speak of *moral subordination* when a person's de facto moral status is in some way less than her/his proper moral status, and where this difference involves some of the basic rights and obligations associated with agent membership in the moral community. Other kinds of subordination can occur with rights appearing at other "levels" of moral theory, but the involvement of these most basic ones has particularly far-reaching consequences.

One form of moral subordination that is generally allowed for in daily life is when there is in the society a common and fairly overt denial of a person's proper moral status. Perhaps there is the general belief that some of the basic rights do not apply to the individual. The refusal to acknowledge these rights may be revealed in some long-standing custom or it may even be enacted into law. For example, at various times laws have denied that children, women, members of certain ethnic groups, and others are persons, thereby denying them a number of the associated basic rights. In some countries, a woman's testimony cannot be admitted into a court proceeding unless it is first corroborated by another, independent, witness. This means that in effect a woman cannot bring charges of assault against her attacker, not unless another person already gives a confirming account. Her right to protest a serious wrong is severely curtailed by law. As a nonlegal example, in many societies there is a long-standing custom of not recognizing a child's right to an apology from an adult when wronged. There is the confused but dismally revealing assumption that for an adult to apologize to a child is demeaning and contrary to the proper relationship between the two. Even when the wrong is clearly recognized, there remains the firm belief that no apology is owed.

But this fairly overt denial of some of the rights or obligations is not the only way in which moral subordination can occur. A person's de facto moral status has two components: the person's generally recognized moral status and what I call the person's *effective moral empowerment*. Roughly, the latter is the power to exercise her basic moral rights, fulfill her basic (prima facie) obligations (such as the obligation to think about moral decision making), and to interact with other members of the moral community in ways that sustain her networks of proper moral relations with them.

My focus is on agent-and-patient members of the moral community whose moral rights include those mentioned above. Such an individual can become morally subordinate via two routes. In the first place, the person's overtly recognized moral status may in some way be less than it should be, or, second, the person may lack effective moral empowerment by being blocked from exercising his/her moral rights or excluded from the kind of interaction that sustains the proper moral relations with others. Sometimes the block can become "internal," and recent literature on oppression has coined the phrase "internalized oppression" for this phenomenon. But in this chapter the focus will be on situations that involve only external blocking.

Both routes are commonly found within civilized oppression, but the lack of moral empowerment is the less visible. Some well-intentioned agents, not themselves victims, have worked against oppression by trying to amend the overtly recognized moral status of the victims. But these reformers have sometimes found themselves baffled as to why such amendments, especially if turned into law, leave the same groups of people marginalized and still oppressed in some way. For nonvictims it is genuinely difficult to see the second route to moral subordination, via the lack of moral empowerment. The sanctions that maintain the disempowerment involve neither physical force nor the use of law. They are therefore difficult to perceive in themselves, and they mask the disempowerment they are sustaining. This difficulty of perception is increased if the agents responsible are without malicious intent, which is more common than not.

I am looking at cases where the morally disempowered are ex hypothesi full moral agents with all the attributes involved. So as individuals they may be very articulate, clear thinking, reflective, and calmly assertive. The socially privileged may not understand how anyone with such attributes could be effectively disempowered morally, except by legal means or sheer force. Surely such qualities are just the ones needed to make an individual appropriately powerful, that is, nonoppressed? If the person's overtly recognized moral status is all that it should be, and if the individual also has the attributes above, what can go wrong? But in Western nations the civilized and nonmalicious moral disempowerment of the targeted groups is precisely how moral subordination usually occurs.

Social privilege plays a major role in this subordination, given the various forms of power the privileged exercise. Those favored with social status regularly call upon subtle but highly effective forms of indirect power, like the consequential power and the suppport power described in chapter 3. And they habitually exercise interactive power in many and varied situations, often far beyond any appropriate level that is attached to any social role they are placed in. Excessive interactive power is especially likely to contribute to civilized oppression. In fact it is remarkably easy for what look like fairly minor differences in interactive power combined with an unintended selectivity to block what should be basic knowledge of the victim and his/her forms of excellence, and to block moral rights, even basic ones like the right to pertinent information, the right to present information and arguments about first-hand encounters with relevant situations, or the right to meaningful protest when seriously wronged. In crucial ways victims are silenced and immobilized. It is not uncommon for a good-hearted, well-intentioned person of privilege to overtly recognize some component of a more vulnerable person's proper moral status, while at the same time unwittingly using the accepted power of the privileged to morally disempower the person in that same respect. Inflicting moral subordination is an ongoing danger for those with varied, extensive, and habitually exercised power.

TWO KINDS OF RESPECT

The set of rights and obligations above embody the most crucial elements of the moral life, something that is naturally associated with being a decisionmaker. They capture not only the individual's commitment to moral inquiry but also the moral community's commitment to sustaining basic moral relations and amending inappropriate relationships when necessary. Indeed, these rights and obligations embody the kind of respect owed to agent members of the moral community.

Many have argued that respect is owed to all moral persons, but when this respect is "cashed out," the kinds of things listed as either duties or appropriate behavior are often either very restricted or rather haphazard. Rawls, for example, in *A Theory of Justice*, speaks of "the [natural] duty . . . to show a person the respect which is due to him as a moral being, that is, as a being with a sense of justice and a conception of the good."[2] He mentions two things: seeing the situation of others "from the perspective of their conception of their good" and also "being prepared to give reasons for our actions whenever the interests of others are materially affected."[3] The second of these duties is much the same as one of the ones I argue for, but I arrive at it as part of a more explicit analysis of the moral life, and I emphasize the role of any major power difference involved and, via this analysis, arrive at a number of other items.

Some other attempts to explain the obligations associated with this respect seem rather haphazard. Gregory Vlastos, in his discussion of justice and equality, is an example. He says that if respect "were applicable *only* in relations of personal love, it would be irrelevant for the analysis of justice,"[4] and refers to "the role of [individuals having] the same value in the moral community."[5] But then he writes that "To be sincere, reliable, fair, kind, tolerant, unintrusive, modest in my relations with my fellows is not due them because they have made brilliant or even passing moral grades, but simply because they happen to be fellow-members of the moral community."[6] These are surely all elements of ordinary, decent behavior, but giving them in this context involves a slide between two uses of the term "respect."

The phrase "respect for a person" has at least two different meanings. The now standard labels for the distinction were introduced by Stephen Darwall in his article "Two Kinds of Respect."[7] On the one hand, the phrase can refer to respect based on moral personhood or membership in the moral community. This respect is standardly described as "unearned," and following Stephen Darwall's label is now often called *recognition respect*. On the other hand, regard that is in response to features and abilities that are special to the individual and not shared by all persons is often described as "earned" (in the relevant sense). Some of this regard involves again moral features of the individual, this time the individual's moral character, and it falls under a second concept of respect, often now called *appraisal respect*, again, following Darwall's label.

Vlastos is clearly referring to recognition respect, respect that is owed to someone even if the appraisal respect owed is virtually nil. That is to say, on this position there is a kind of respect owed equally to the sadistic serial murderer as to the selfless individual who conceals a Jewish family from the German SS. But it is not clear that we do owe the serial murderer anything like "kindness" (in any positive sense over and above that of refraining from cruelty) or "reliability," to take two of Vlastos's examples.

It is even less clear that we are duty bound to be "unintrusive," and I would argue that we in fact have a duty *not* to be "tolerant." That is to say, Vlastos's list of the kinds of actions that reflect recognition respect looks plausible only if we tacitly think just of people who, like most people, deserve a significant degree of appraisal respect.

If recognition respect is indeed morally appropriate, it would of course be owed to individuals not in "relations of personal love," to use Vlastos's phrase. Certainly the actions he lists may be appropriate beyond our dealings with those close to us. But some of them may be inappropriate for another reason, namely, the unusually low degree of appraisal respect owed to the person in question. The test case for his list of actions is not simply the possibility of a complete stranger, but the possibility of a justifiably almost nonexistent degree of appraisal respect.

The usual move is to insist that the individuals are intrinsically valuable even if their moral character and their actions are horrendous. Vlastos himself speaks of their "intrinsic value as individual human beings,"[8] but the attempt to ground this intrinsic value in something shared by all humans, or at least all persons, is not easy. On the other hand it isn't difficult to argue that the set of basic rights and obligations referred to in this work do apply to at least all agent members of the moral community, regardless of their actions and moral character, and they give shape to what basic moral relations ought to be like. And if those rights and obligations embody a type of respect, then it is a respect that should be afforded to even the worst of moral offenders. That is to say, we are referring to recognition respect.

MORAL PERSONHOOD AND SELF-RESPECT

In the rest of this chapter I wish to say something about the connection between self-respect and this set of rights and obligations. Victims of wrongdoing and injustice are often urged to maintain their self-respect regardless of how they are being treated, but there are limits to a victim's control over self-respect, and in particular, limits that are not due to the person's psychological resources. I will argue that a victim may steadfastly refuse to cooperate with a pattern of received injustice and the associated attack on self-respect and yet be unable to sustain self-respect.

We need first to do some minimal sorting out of terminology. In fairly recent literature on self-respect the terminology varies. The distinctions found there do not carve up the conceptual territory in one consistent way, but the one that is widely shared parallels Darwall's distinction (above) between recognition respect and appraisal respect. Roughly, self-valuing or self-regard based on moral personhood is described as "unearned" and is a form of self-respect now often called "recognition self-respect." On the other hand, some self-regard is dependent on features and abilities that are special to the individual rather than shared by all persons. This self-regard takes two different forms. Some of this "earned" self-regard concerns moral attributes, specifically, the individual's moral character, and falls under a second concept of self-respect, often now called "appraisal self-respect." But much of the "earned" self-regard involves the development and attainments of nonmoral attributes and abilities and is standardly called "self-esteem." Although a few writers use "self-respect" and "self-esteem" interchangeably (such as Kant in *Lectures on Ethics* [standard translations] and Rawls in *A Theory of Justice*), the distinction is useful and increasingly familiar. Both self-respect and self-esteem are morally important, but some different issues are involved. The focus here is on one of the forms of self-respect, namely, recognition self-respect, which is based on moral personhood rather than individual moral character.

It has traditionally been claimed that we "owe all persons respect" because of their shared moral status as persons, regardless of more individual features and abilities, and that consequently all persons should respect themselves. The moral status that grounds the recognition self-respect sometimes refers to the "intrinsic value" of persons, but far more usually in current work, the grounds refer to "certain basic moral rights." Laurence Thomas, for example, writes that "a person has self-respect, I shall say, if and only if he has the conviction that he is deserving of full moral status, and so the basic rights of that status, simply in virtue of the fact that he is a person."[9]

MORAL PERSONHOOD: THE INDIVIDUAL MODEL

Centering the concept of self-respect around moral personhood and basic rights and obligations that attach to it is, I believe, a well-grounded move. That will be obvious from the work so far. But quite often the concept of moral personhood called upon is oversimplifed. It is based on a description of the individual as an isolated unit. Elizabeth Wolgast is just one of a number of philosophers dissatisfied with what she calls this "social atomism" approach to moral issues.[10] She argues that this understanding of society makes it difficult to find a place for "friendliness or sympathy," for example.[11] On this model we think of society as "made up of individual people, as bricks in a wall, as molecules in a substance"; "they are "complete and real, each in him- or herself."[12] Or again, as Iris Marion Young notes, with this model, individuals are conceived as "social atoms, logically prior to social relations and institutions."[13]

The standard concept of moral personhood is similarly atomistic. It is built around a description of the (adult) individual with the usual capacities: being able to imagine situations, think about problems, remember past actions, make reflective decisions, and so on. Moral persons have these abilities, and thereby have some basic moral rights (and obligations). On this standard account, to have *full moral status* is to be an individual who has these capacities and rights. The basic features and rights of the static individual are all one needs to be aware of to know that someone has moral personhood, and self-respect is a matter of believing one has these capacities and rights and valuing oneself because of them.

I have already argued that when it comes to actually stating what these rights are, the list is quite often either too restricted or rather haphazard. But now I wish to address a different problem. Although I believe that moral personhood does involve some basic rights, still, if we mistakenly construe "moral person" solely via the model of a static individual, then we tacitly adopt a general understanding of what a right is that is badly flawed. When that understanding is modified, we will find that sometimes calls upon victims to maintain their self-respect are, in fact, unreasonable, regardless of how robust their psychological resources.

The standard way of talking about rights *assigns* rights to individuals. Some individuals may have *more* rights than others. In a significant sense, rights are things that individuals "have" or possess, yet of course they involve more than the individual who "has" them. At most on the traditional view, the involvement of others is acknowledged by speaking of rights as place holders for *claims* the individual can make against others. Again, a compatible philosopher here is Young, who is just as dissatisfied with this way of talking about rights: "Rights are not fruitfully conceived as possessions. Rights are relationships, not things; they are institutionally defined rules specifying what people can do in relation to one another. Rights refer to doing more than to having, to social relationships that enable or constrain action."[14] As a political philosopher, Young focuses primarily on justice issues "on the grand scale," particularly the limitations of the distributive model of social justice. With our present interest in moral personhood and self-respect, many kinds of relationships are relevant since those that can sustain or damage a person's moral status include not only those between the individual and members of influential institutions (in the usual use of the word "institution"), but also more personal relationships.

MORAL PERSONHOOD: THE FUNCTIONING MEMBER MODEL

The traditional way of construing rights is very compatible with the "static, individual" model of moral personhood, but it is particularly inappropriate when speaking of the basic rights in question—those set out in the earlier part of this chapter. It is vital to the moral status of (agent) members of the moral community that they have the associated rights and obligations. Standardly this has meant checking that they have the relevant basic capacities, and concluding that they therefore have the relevant rights. But to be a full member of the moral community is to be able to *function* in certain ways. Certainly some of the "being able" is to do with the individual's own characteristics, but it's a shadowy and insubstantial kind of "being able" if the basic functioning is systematically blocked in serious ways, if the person's de facto moral status is not what it should be. And this can occur in either of the two ways mentioned earlier: either by overtly denying some component of the person's proper moral status (perhaps by denying that some of the rights apply to the individual), or by formally acknowledging the individual's proper moral status while at the same time systematically preventing its actualization. For example, a person may have the basic moral rights in name only, being routinely blocked from exercising them. A person does not need all relationships to be perfectly sustaining in order to have full moral status. On the other hand, the person does not have that status when trapped in quite a number of morally inappropriate relationships that involve systematic moral disempowerment. The person is blocked from functioning appropriately within the moral community, and this has implications for the issue of self-respect.

Recent literature does contain material on the importance of institutions and social relationships for self-respect. In *A Theory of Justice* Rawls claims it is "necessary . . . that there should be for each person at least one community of shared interests to which he belongs and where he finds his endeavors confirmed by his associates."[15] Laurence Thomas points out that if there is any group whose members "share the same biological or social characteristics" and which falls almost entirely within the larger group of people lacking self-respect in that society, then this indicates that the social institutions are not arranged as they should be.[16] They are fairly arranged "if and only if from the standpoint of such institutions everyone is justified in having the beliefs for which self-respect calls,"[17] beliefs about the rights involved in the "full moral status" associated with being a person. And there are a good number of other such references.

The importance of social relationships for self-respect is something I fully endorse. For too long self-respect has been thought of as entirely within the individual's control. When Kant, for example, comments on self-respect and related concepts, the general tenor of his writing projects a tacit and fairly unrelenting assumption of perpetual individual control over the relevant acts, beliefs, and responses. He writes: "We are not indifferent to cringing servility; man should not cringe and fawn; by so doing he degrades his person and loses his manhood."[18] It seems that no matter what happens, no matter what situation people find themselves in, they are to be "blamed" for certain kinds of responses.

> . . . the faint-hearted who complain about their luck and sigh and weep about their misfortunes are despicable in our eyes; instead of sympathizing with them we do our best to keep away from them. But if a man shows a steadfast courage in his misfortune, and though greatly suffering does not cringe and complain but puts a bold face upon things, to such a one our sympathy goes out.[19]

(This is not someone to have a beer with when you've just lost your job.)

> A rational man . . . should not disavow the moral self-esteem [i.e., self-respect] of such a being, that is, he should pursue his end, which is in itself a duty, not abjectly, not in a servile spirit as if he were seeking a favor, . . . but always with consciousness of his sublime moral predisposition. . . . And this self-esteem [i.e., self-respect] is a duty of man to himself.[20]

The general impression is that it's all a matter of the individual's decision, and that the person is therefore at fault for servile behavior or for failing in this "duty" of self-respect. The recent insistence on the influence of social relationships is a welcome antidote to this exaggerated portrayal of individual control.

INTERNAL AND EXTERNAL BLOCKING

But I wish to distinguish two different ways in which self-respect can be lost. For simplicity, I will refer to them as "internal" and "external" blocking of the person's proper functioning in the moral community, since these two terms capture something crucial about how the two ways differ. I will look first at internal blocking.

Sometimes certain unsound relationships or institutions can causally affect the self-image individuals hold and also their beliefs about their proper moral status. The beliefs may be accurate or false, and similarly the self-image may be either morally sound or a morally degrading. There can be, then, a causal connection between the relationships and a distorted "mental" item produced (the belief, the self-image), and this in turn can result in a loss of self-respect. Perhaps, for example, the individual is wrongly convinced that, being unemployed and desperately poor, he is socially "unimportant" and has no right to address "important" people—like famous politicians discussing welfare cuts—and "take up their valuable time" by trying to give accurate information on what inescapable poverty involves. Or perhaps the individual has been trained to believe that, being a woman, she has no right to protest, no matter how much contempt her husband displays in his treatment of her, since a woman's proper role is to "stand by her husband no matter what."

Once acquired, such inaccurate beliefs and conceptions can function to oppress the individual "from within," which is usually described as "internalized oppression." Sandra Bartky notes that,

> The possession of autonomy . . . is widely thought to distinguish persons from non-persons; but some female stereotypes . . . threaten the autonomy of women. Oppressed people might or might not be in a position to exercise their autonomy, but the psychologically oppressed may come to believe that they lack the capacity to be autonomous whatever their position.[21]

The concept of internalized oppression is surely one of the most insightful additions to the conceptual tools for dealing with injustice and oppression, but I am cautious about locating its boundaries.

In cases like the denigrated wife and the unemployed individual in poverty, the person lacks appropriate beliefs about his/her proper moral status, and also the person's moral self is blocked from functioning properly as a member of the moral community—but the block, it seems, has become internal. Often *victim-directed* suggestions are made: the person should join a support group, should take "assertiveness training," should seek therapy, and so on. The goal is to intervene in the causal chain between the relationships and the internalized oppression by replacing the inaccurate beliefs or self-conceptions with those that are robustly correct, so that self-respect is restored.

The removal of any such internal block is, of course, a necessary condition for self-respect, but something important is being overlooked here if we think this will reliably bring about restoration of self-respect. Removing that block is a necessary, but by no means sufficient, condition for achieving the goal.

If in fact it is only a relatively insignificant portion of a person's relationship network that causally triggers the internal block, and the rest of the relationships are basically sound, then indeed victim-directed intervention may be effective in breaking the causal chain, removing the inner block, thereby restoring appropriate functioning and self-respect. (What counts as an insignificant portion will vary. Sometimes one or two major relationships right at the center of someone's life may constitute a significant portion. Sometimes quite a number of relationships are peripheral and insignificant, even taken all together.) Once the inner block is removed, ex hypothesi there is nothing to prevent the person's proper functioning in general.

However, there is a second way in which self-respect can be blocked, which is "external" in a particularly crucial sense. Certainly having a secure conviction of the relevant beliefs is one vital component of full self-respect, but it is not sufficient, not if we take seriously the conception of the moral self as a functioning member of the moral community. As we have seen, various writers appreciate the dependence of self-respect on the recognition of one's rights as a member of the moral community, but we will find that this account needs to be supplemented by the awareness of a further aspect of one's moral status. This includes one's socially determined ability or inability to exercise the rights and fulfill the obligations of a fully functioning member. When the functioning is "externally blocked," as I call it, then while there is no diminution of the individual's moral rights, they cannot be fully actualized. Typically, also, one cannot adequately fulfill the basic obligations that attach to membership, and so cannot be effectively called upon in those respects. The proper moral status remains unchanged, but the person cannot take up his/her full moral role. In serious ways the blocked individual is sidelined.

I have argued that being trapped in a web of relationships that systematically blocks the person in these kinds of ways, is to be *externally* blocked from functioning as a moral self (that is, as someone with the basic moral rights and obligations in more than name only). The relationships a person is in, whether institutional or more personal, need to be predominantly sound before the person's proper and de facto moral status coincide, before the person *has* the functioning moral self that is the object of full self-respect. We are no longer speaking simply about a causal chain between distorted social relationships and distorted beliefs, which function as an inner block to proper functioning, and thereby produce a loss of self-respect. If the individual's relationship network is extensively unsound, and if the individual is relatively powerless compared with those who are the prime controllers of the relationships, then the properly functioning self cannot be realized no matter how accurate the individual's beliefs. The self as an appropriately functioning member of the moral community is the proper object of self-respect, or so I have argued, but this is not an attainable condition in these circumstances. No matter how appropriate the individual's inner condition (the beliefs and attitude), the person remains externally blocked from having full self-respect. For this reason perhaps we can say that the connection between appropriate social relationships and self-respect is stronger than is usually realized: they form one constituent without which full self-respect is impossible.

Oversights about this revictimize the victims. In the first place, even if there are self-denigrating beliefs and attitudes, it is a serious mistake to assume that successful removal of that inner block will restore full self-respect. It restores one vital component, but whether or not this is sufficient for self-respect depends on the individual's relationships and level of power within them. For victims who have struggled to overcome such internal barriers, it can be a painful and slow-dawning realization that the outcome they had been led to expect is still somehow out of their reach.

In the second place, when there is no internal block and yet full self-respect is not attainable, bystanders who do not grasp the constitutive role of the individual's relationships predictably insist that the problem *is* internal to the victim. There has to be some inner barrier, however subtle its form. They do not perceive the external blocking of the victim's proper functioning that comes from the distorted relationships, and the victim is "blamed" for lacking robust self-respect. These victim-blaming incidents usually belong in Category 3 of those examined in the previous chapter: there is in fact moral harm (because of the morally unsound relationships), but then all moral responsibility of the actual agents (those controlling the relationships) is dismissed by the claim that the harm is nonmoral. In this case, the harm is usually thought of as natural because the lack of self-respect is believed to exist because of unfortunate psychological failings of the victim. As mentioned in the earlier chapter, this kind of victim blaming can be objectionable in more than one way. The attributions of such failings, even though false, bring embarrassment and humiliation, and the suggestion that the solution is, in principle at least, in the hands of the victim is a cruel illusion for victims who believe it and an infuriating piece of deflection for victims who are fully alert to the controlling relationships.

If all this is acknowledged, it may still be objected that although relationships *could* constrain an individual so much that his/her de facto moral status was seriously degraded, this could only be by physical force or the use of law, which would now be a relatively unusual occurrence in Western societies. So if someone is not functioning as a full moral self, it is nearly always something more internal to the individual. In response to this, I have articulated earlier (in chapter 3) forms of power that involve neither physical force nor the use of law and that can be very effectively used to distort what should be the basic moral relations holding between members of the moral community, and this in ways that systematically block some individuals from exercising certain rights even when those rights are openly acknowledged. These relationships are relatively easy to impose on the less powerful members of society, and for anyone who is systematically oppressed, it is impossible to simply "decide to change" those relationships for a whole new set free from such distortions.

Those in such a situation can have a robust sense of their own worth as an isolated individual, and have all the right beliefs about their proper moral status, and yet for very good reason lack full self-respect. If the con straining relationships depend on social rather than physical or legal power, then often the *ongoing* role they play is not perceived by onlookers. The lack of self-respect is construed as having a purely internal basis, and the usual victim-directed solutions are urged. The problem, however, does not lie in the moral character, psychological condition, or beliefs of the victim, but in the fact that the object of full self-respect—the functioning moral self—cannot be actualized because of externally imposed constraints. The lack of self-respect is obviously a bad thing, and yet in one way the person's awareness of it is not, since it displays discernment, a resilience of mind and character in resisting any tempting self-deception about how degraded one's moral status is, and how powerless one is to change it (in the cases referred to).

For any individual adult with the usual abilities to think, remember, imagine, decide, and so on, it is crucial that the vast majority of their relationships permit the functioning of the moral self. Indeed, the relationships most under social control, especially those involving influential social institutions, should do more and actually promote the functioning of the moral self of those under the sphere of their influence. This cannot guarantee that people will have self-respect, since there can be internal hindrances to their having an appropriate mental attitude, but I am indeed arguing for the necessary contribution of morally appropriate relations with other members of the moral community.

Sandra Bartky is surely right when she claims that "oppression . . . is ordinarily conceived in too limited a fashion,"[22] but the options Bartky offers seem themselves too limited. She writes that "it is possible to be oppressed in ways that need involve neither physical deprivation, legal inequality, nor economic exploitation; one can be oppressed psychologically. . . . [which] can be regarded as the 'internalization of intimations of inferiority.' "[23] But this moves too quickly from "not oppressed physically, legally, or economically" to "internally oppressed." The situation I am considering need involve no internalized oppression. The relationships, given the trend they exhibit, constitute socially structured contempt of the victims, and both the constrained relations themselves, and also the associated lack of full self-respect are mechanisms of oppression, however unintentional.

Recognition self-respect is by no means the only kind of self-regard. It deals only with *some* aspects of the self that are shared by most humans. Self-esteem, for example, covers a range of other, nonmoral aspects of the self. However, if things are badly wrong with the kind of matters involved in recognition self-respect, it is difficult for other kinds of matters to go well. For several reasons I agree with Thomas that "self-respect is a more fundamental sense of worth than self-esteem."[24] Similarly, when speaking of respect and regard owed to each other, recognition respect refers to just one basic matter. It is based on moral personhood, which, as I construe it, means the proper functioning of the moral self in the moral community. So it is crucial for agent members of the community.

This conception of moral personhood has a seemingly radical implication for recognition respect from others, which should be acknowledged.[25] We have already seen that since this conception centers around being fully functioning members of the moral community, individuals can fail to be paradigm members and can fall short of full moral agency, for reasons that are socially imposed. Although some very basic moral rights and the belief that one has them are necessary to self-respect, I have argued that there is also a crucial social component, that the conditions for full self-respect involve relationships that may lie beyond the individual's control. The implication for recognition respect from others is that the parallel point holds. The appropriate object of full recognition respect is a fully functioning member of the moral community, and someone who is extensively oppressed is not able to function appropriately. He may not protest, even when seriously wronged, may not ask for information he is entitled to, may not give pertinent first-hand information to powerful decision makers, may not correct the distorted public self that the local community has fixed on him, may readily not be well placed to support fellow victims of oppressive relationships, and so on. This does not constitute the kind of appropriately functioning member that is the proper object of full recognition respect from others, and the special evil of civilized oppression is that the responsibility of powerful others in all of this is largely invisible. The victims themselves are often blamed for the lack of full recognition respect they receive.

When people are oppressed in this way, it remains the case that in virtue of their personal characteristics, they have all the basic moral rights of members. There is no question as to the injustice of their position, or the moral imperative to restore them to the full exercise of their rights. Is recognition respect owed to them? There is some degree of ambiguity in the question. In the immediate situation, full recognition respect, whether from oneself or from others, cannot be given to a fully functioning member if there is no such object. That is the parallel that holds between self-respect and respect from others. But there is a second, morally crucial, sense in which recognition respect is most definitely owed to them. It is clearly called for by their proper moral status, and that is precisely why their social situation and the resulting de facto moral status are morally intolerable.

There is, of course, far more to people than what is involved in this type of respect. There is also appraisal respect, which is based on moral character, and there is all that falls under "esteem," including the whole array of fascinating features, characteristics, and talents people have, with any degree of individual particularity and uniqueness. For anyone who believes that the moral community includes some nonagent members, some who are patients only, there is a wealth of grounds available for arguing that regard is owed to them, even though they are not "moral persons" in the agent-member sense.

THE ROLE OF RIGHTS

Before leaving this chapter, I wish to suggest that the principles set out in it go a long way to answering some otherwise legitimate concerns about the central role played by rights here. Traditionally, the most frequent contenders for the label of "basic rights" have been the rights to life, liberty, and property, all construed as negative rights. For this reason one can sympathize with the kinds of concerns that Robin Dillon raises in her article, "Toward a Feminist Conception of Self-Respect." She writes, for example, that "insofar as persons are viewed as essentially rights-bearers, we are separated and distanced from each other. For many of our fundamental moral rights function as barriers to protect us from the encroachments of others, and to respect a person's rights is to keep one's distance from her."[26] She also writes that ". . . an exclusive or even a strong emphasis on respecting ourselves as rights-bearers does not offer us a way of viewing and valuing ourselves that could serve as the basis for the transformation of society along more integrative lines."[27]

Dillon's comments about rights as "barriers" are quite justified so long as we think of the traditional "basic rights," but whether it is a fair comment about rights as such depends on how rights are construed and which rights one has in mind. When rights are construed in the standard way, almost like possessions, and we restrict those rights to the few, traditional negative rights, then this will predictably result in a society of "atoms," each minding his/her own business so far as possible. But we need not reject the role of rights out of hand because of this.

Construing rights in the way I have above, together with the nature of some of those rights, means that we have moral obligations to actively construct social relations—both institutional and more personal—in ways that promote the exercise of those rights. This would involve reviewing many social practices, not just "big scale" matters but also small yet influential blocking mechanisms found in apparently trivial social conventions. A strong emphasis on these rights would indeed involve "transforming" a number of deeply entrenched patterns found in Western societies.

Furthermore, it would not involve generally adversarial relationships—contrary to first impressions. For example, relationships constructed to allow genuinely meaningful protest from the more vulnerable would lack intimidation even though some parties might have more power and responsibility. But when relationships are transformed in such ways, people ask questions, raise concerns, and sort out misunderstandings at an early stage, before anger is entrenched. There is less antagonism when the rights are taken seriously, not more.

The principles given call for active involvement in constructing appropriate relationships between agent members of the moral community. Some relationships will of course involve more. There is no attempt here to argue for every appropriate feature of every kind of relationship. That would be work on a scale far beyond any book. And the focus has, in any case, been on those who are agents, since their individual abilities and capacities can mask their vulnerability. It is here that civilized oppression goes most easily unnoticed, and the basic rights and obligations referred to provide insights into how such oppression gets a hold on the daily lives of its victims. As we have seen, much of the oppression occurs within institutional settings where the contributing agents have institutional roles. So in the final chapter I will mention just a few of the most relevant points about the moral accountability of the midsized institutions that have so large a role in structuring social life.

NOTES

1. J. Harvey, "Forgiving as an Obligation of the Moral Life," *International Journal of Moral and Social Studies* 8, no. 3 (Autumn 1993): 211–22.

2. John Rawls, *A Theory of Justice* (Cambridge, Mass.: Harvard University Press, 1971), 337.

3. Rawls, 337.

4. Gregory Vlastos, "Justice and Equality," in *Social Justice*, ed. Richard Brandt (Englewood Cliffs, N.J.: Prentice-Hall, 1962), 45.

5. Vlastos, 47.

6. Vlastos, 47.

7. Stephen Darwall, "Two Kinds of Respect," *Ethics* 88, no. 1 (October 1977): 36–49.

8. Vlastos, 48.

9. Laurence Thomas, "Self-Respect: Theory and Practice," in *Philosophy Born of Struggle: Anthology of Afro-American Philosophy from 1917*, ed. Leonard Harris (Dubuque, Iowa: Kendall/Hunt, 1983), 175–76.

10. Elizabeth H. Wolgast, *The Grammar of Justice* (Ithaca, N.Y.: Cornell University Press, 1987).

11. Wolgast, 25–26.

12. Wolgast, 10–11.

13. Iris Marion Young, *Justice and the Politics of Difference* (Princeton: Princeton University Press, 1990), 27.

14. Young, 25.

15. Rawls, 442.

16. Thomas, 185.

17. Thomas, 184–85.

18. Immanuel Kant, *Lectures on Ethics*, trans. Louis Infield (New York: Harper & Row, 1963), 118.

19. Kant, *Lectures on Ethics*, 119.

20. Immanuel Kant, *The Metaphysics of Morals*, trans. Mary Gregor (Cambridge: Cambridge University Press, 1991), 230–31.

21. Sandra L. Bartky, *Femininity and Domination* (New York: Routledge, 1990), 29–30.

22. Bartky, 29.

23. Bartky, 22.

24. Thomas, 182.

25. I am grateful to the publisher's referee for pointing out the parallel here between (recognition) self-respect and recognition respect from others.

26. Robin S. Dillon, "Toward a Feminist Conception of Self-Respect," *Hypatia* 7, no. 1 (Winter 1992): 52–69, 57.

27. Dillon, 58.

Chapter 7

Personnel Relations

Because so many of our moral relationships arise from the institutions or professions we take part in, we need to consider two kinds of issues. The first kind concerns the possible conflicts in accomodating our institutional or social roles and obligations within our basic role as a member of the moral community. The second kind of issue concerns the accountability of midsized institutions for their wrongdoing, and the importance of reestablishing appropriate moral relations within the institution afterward. To help illustrate some of the central points, I will consider the slowly emerging practice of public, institutional apologies, where some member of an institution offers apologies on behalf of that institution.

I will first explore some interconnections between membership in the moral community and membership in some institution or profession and look at some implications for morality in the wider sense, that is, not restricted to this or that institutional context.

ROLE-DEFINED VERSUS ORDINARY OBLIGATIONS

What makes us moral agents are the normal human capacities of deciding, acting, reflecting, interacting with others, revising our views, and so on. The work of moral endeavor is just part of living the human life. What does that mean for someone in a specific social role? Suppose someone has a professional or institutional role. Standardly there will be some special relationships associated with the role, and some role-attached obligations. For example, a salesperson in a store has some prima facie obligations to the customers because of that role. He should try to help the customer locate the desired item, assist the customer courteously, ensure that the correct change is given, and so on. It is not unusual for some of these role obligations to be supportable via an alternative route if they are arguably straightforward moral obligations anyway (perhaps like the duty to give the correct change), while others would not be supportable independently of the associated role (like the obligation to help the customer locate the desired item). But even though a set of role obligations may include an interestingly mixed set of items in this kind of way, still, focusing solely on special role-relationships can lead to moral oversights in common practices and beliefs.

In the first place, the people involved in those relationships may be owed other obligations that do not stem from the role in question. Consider the salesperson again. If a customer leaves the counter with a parting comment about "catching the Downtown bus outside," and the salesperson knows there are no buses on that street at that time in the evening, he should call after the customer and explain, rather than watch her go to wait futilely, especially fairly late in the evening. But this is not related to the role held. A fellow customer standing at the counter has the same obligation. It is only ordinary decency to try to prevent an unpleasant, frustrating, and possibly unsafe situation. The same underlying point can be made for many other institutional or professional roles: while someone is in the social role, obligations can arise to the people in the special, associated relationships that, however, do not stem from the role and those relationships.

Second, it is a common view in society at large that if someone is a member of an institution or profession, and if the goals of the institution or profession are morally neutral or even morally desirable, then while in that role, all the person has to think about morally are the obligations attached to the role. With this exclusive focus on the relevant special relationships, it is natural to conclude that the individuals involved in those relationships always have first claim to consideration. It may even be held that they have the only claim to moral consideration while one is in the institutional role. This may look innocuous, given that the goals of the profession or institution are ex hypothesi not morally objectionable. It may seem especially safe in the case of the caring professions, like those of medicine or social work, but even here the assumption leads to moral problems.

For example, some doctors have supported unthinkingly cruel means toward serving their patients, including very painful experiments on vulnerable groups who happen not to be their patients, such as prisoners, institutionalized mentally challenged people, children in state-run orphanages, and countless thousands of defenseless animals. Any claim that it is not the doctors' responsibility to be concerned about those who are not their patients reflects a naive conception of the moral responsibility attached to membership in the moral community. Nor is it true that somebody else is bound to step in and defend the interests of the vulnerable. The documented abuse of the powerless makes long and dismal reading, and recorded abuse is but a portion of the whole.

Sometimes when professions have embraced the mistake of believing that only their role obligations have a call upon them while they are in their professional role, the resulting situations have been so disturbing to the general public that eventually legal intervention has been brought to bear. In some places, for example, psychiatrists are required to report active child abusers who are their clients. What is most relevant here is not the specific moral claim that protection of abused children takes moral precedence over the standard confidentiality between psychiatrist and patient, but rather the claim that we cannot legitimately just set aside our ordinary moral obligations when we move into a specific social or professional or institutional role. It is possible, therefore, that some innocuous looking role obligation may turn out to be morally unsound once we look beyond the boundaries of that role, something incumbent on any agent member of the moral community.

Again, in many places lawyers are required, by their professional governing body, never to advise their clients against their interests. On the face of it, it looks quite proper, and in practice it will function in a morally appropriate fashion most of the time. But consider a possible case like the following (based on one reported to have actually occurred). A vehicle made by a major car manufacturer has a potentially lethal design flaw. Parents whose child dies as a result of this problem sue the manufacturers. Their lawyer establishes that there is abundant evidence that the company knew of the danger. The company offers to settle out of court, but only if the parents legally bind themselves not to disclose anything about the case, the charges, or the settlement to anyone in the future. The parents are morally concerned by this condition, since they believe that without publicity about the death and the cause, the problem in the vehicle will not be fixed, and other families will go through the agony of an unnecessary death. Their own immediate interests will be best served by accepting the company's offer: the money will be immediately received, it will eliminate any risk of losing the case in court, and they will be spared the huge expenses and the extended further strain connected with an actual court case—all of which their lawyer points out. When they explain their deep and persistent moral concern about the suppression of the facts, their lawyer expresses understanding and support, and advises them to act as their conscience directs.

Even though the parents fully understand their options and initiate the proposal to forgo the out-of-court settlement, the lawyer is brought up on charges by his professional association for advising his clients to do what is not in their best interests to do. Not only is the lawyer not permitted to suggest that the couple have overriding obligations to others who use the

same kind of vehicle, he is also not permitted to endorse the already exist-
ing moral position of his clients if it conflicts with their immediate or material self-interest. If such measures were actually taken against a lawyer
in this situation, it amounted to giving an extreme priority to the special
relationships, considerably past the point where a genuine moral di-
lemma first arose.

This extreme priority can show itself in other ways. Sometimes fulfilling one's immediate role obligations has wider, long-range implications
of a morally disturbing kind, all firmly set aside unexplored when this
oversimplified priority is at work. Conrad Brunk in his paper, "Professionalism and Responsibility in the Technological Society," writes of a
professional who "seemed able to view his own participation in the project in isolation from the larger system of which his role was an integral
part."[1] He cites as examples an astronaut's participation in a space mis-
sion that had clear military aspects entirely disowned by the astronaut[2]
and scientists who gave their skills to the development of the atom bomb.[3]

As Beth Savan notes, professional bodies are largely autonomous and,
as a result, "professional bodies appear to feel responsible primarily to
their peers rather than to the wider lay community that they serve."[4] Referring to moral responsibility in the wider sense, not confined to specific
role obligations, Brunk is concerned with "the way the individuals in
these situations find ways to escape moral choice and moral responsibility altogether."[5] He concludes that "it is this escape from any sense of
[moral] responsibility that is one of the most significant aspects of the morality of our age."[6] He is surely correct in noting that this suppression of
all but one's role obligations for the time that one is in the role is increasingly widespread.

A contributing factor here is an unrealistic conception of the nature and
function of "codes of ethics," many of which have been developed in the
last few decades. A code of ethics is drawn up for some specific institution
or profession, and the focus is entirely, or nearly entirely, on situations
and decisions that arise within that context. As with role obligations generally, not all of the obligations set out in such a code are genuinely
moral. Codes of ethics often contain nonmoral matters of etiquette, as
well as statements of conventional procedures. Where guidelines involving moral issues are included, their grounding in wider and more fundamental moral principles is sketchy at best, and there is often little or no
attempt to secure theoretical consistency. Sometimes there are little more
than commonplace sayings to guide institutional members in their decisions involving anyone outside of that context, if indeed any such decisions are referred to in the code.

But then, we should not expect too much from specific codes of ethics.
They were never meant to be a substitute for the lifelong endeavor of

moral inquiry. A fundamental moral principle will necessarily be in terminology more general than most of the wording found in particular
codes of ethics, since a fundamental principle has to serve as guidance in
a vast range of decisionmaking situations, not just those relevant to the
one institutional or professional context. Nor are wider moral principles
dispensable, since, for one thing, it is by appealing to them that we show
the overall goals of an institution or profession to be morally desirable or
at least morally neutral.

THE PRIORITY OF MORALITY PER SE

The view that, while in some special role, we need consider only the obligations attached to that role, is a strange view in that it implies that morality per se is relevant only when we are not in some specific role. If this
is extended to include social roles like being a parent or spouse, then for
some people there may be hardly any time when they are role free. They
are either in an employment-related role, in a family-related role, or
asleep. Only brief and chance encounters with others would qualify for
the most fundamental moral consideration, which is surely a bizarre
view. In short, we do not step out of "the moral community" when we
step into the role of institutional agent, or professional, or family member.

It is not that rare for an obligation grounded in morality as such to take
priority over a specific role obligation, especially given the more or less
restricted scope of any social role. There have been people who have taken
their roles very seriously, who nonetheless have systematically violated
some role obligation on precisely this basis. Both judges and members of
juries, by their very roles, are required to uphold the law and apply it
impartially, but in England in the nineteenth century they refused to do
so. Capital punishment was the penalty for quite a number of offenses,
including forgery and theft of property over a certain value. But both
judges and juries believed it was morally reprehensible to hang someone
for either offense. No matter what was stolen, therefore, many juries routinely assessed the value of the stolen property at one shilling less than
the amount needed to make it a capital offense. They also gave a "not
guilty" verdict whenever someone was brought before them on a charge
of forgery, regardless of the evidence against the person. These role violations could occur over a period of many years and in a widespread fashion only with the support of the judges, who routinely violated their own
role-specific obligation to instruct the jury to uphold the law. Instead, they
managed to convey their support for a false assessment of stolen property
or for a "not guilty" verdict in the case of forgery. The nonconviction of

forgers was so systematic that bankers from 214 cities and towns presented a petition to parliament. It read:

> That your petitioners, as bankers, are deeply interested in the protection of property, from forgery, and in the infliction of punishment on persons guilty of that crime.
>
> That your petitioners find, by experience, that the infliction of death, or even the possibility of the infliction of death, prevents the prosecution, conviction and punishment of the criminal and thus endangers the property which it is intended to protect.
>
> That your petitioners, therefore, earnestly pray that your honorable House will not withhold from them that protection to their property which they would derive from a more lenient law.[7]

As another example, a few individual Roman Catholic priests scattered throughout Europe during the Second World War violated their role obligations by forging baptismal certificates. They gave them to Jewish people to conceal their identity and protect them from murder.

THE INTERNAL FUNCTIONING OF INSTITUTIONS

Such role violations require moral courage, particularly if most fellow institutional agents or professionals wash their hands of the matter and stick strictly to their role obligations. Although the judges formed a majority within their profession, the Catholic priests who forged baptismal documents were far more isolated, and this is the more frequent situation. Institutions, of course, have an interest in focusing only on their own goals and associated obligations. As Smith and Carroll write in a paper on organizational ethics, organizations tend to "resolve internal conflicts between 'business as usual' and a higher level of morality in such a way that the organization's affairs, as these are understood by its leaders, do not seriously suffer."[8] They go on to say that "in a multitude of ways the concentration of power toward the top of the organization is able . . . to help members be 'moral cowards' where the organizations's affairs are involved."[9]

These affairs include both internal matters and also conflicts between the organization's normal workings and the requirements of morality per se. With respect to both kinds of matters, the abdication of moral responsibility by institutional agents often occurs when otherwise valuable aspects of institutional functioning become distorted or are given a priority that is morally untenable. It is particularly likely to occur when efficiency is overemphasized or the concept of loyalty is bent out of shape.

Loyalty of course has responsible and acceptable forms, but it can easily deteriorate into self-protective conformity and the nonexercise of judgment. The moral inadequacy of appealing to such flawed forms of loyalty in defense of an immoral act is clearly established in the literature (such as in recent work by Michalos, and by Bird and Gandz[10]). A distorted concept of loyalty and an overemphasis on efficiency have a predictable impact on the functioning of an institution: dissent is suppressed, protest and even the raising of concerns are blocked, explanations and justification of decisions by the more powerful are not given, and there is an "upward only" accountability in that people see themselves as answerable only to yet more powerful institutional members. These things all nurture a loss of a sense of moral responsibility, and as a result, the response to the requirements of morality per se suffers, whether those requirements concern issues that are internal or external to the institution.

Since we do not step out of the moral community when we step into the role of institutional agent, professional, or family member, the basic prima facie rights and obligations mentioned in the previous chapter are retained by institutional agents and others in their social roles. These include the right to protest and call for the amendment of serious wrongs, the right of bystanders to intervene on behalf of vulnerable victims, the obligation to review, revise, and try to extend our moral understanding, and the right to present to each other information and arguments expected to help in this. They include also the right to hear the justifications for power-backed decisions that significantly affect our lives and, if the moral relationship is basically sound, the obligation to take any concern first to the agent who seems to be the most responsible. These rights and obligations provide some guidelines for screening the basic internal functioning of institutions.

In the first place, they should be recognized and acknowledged, and in many institutions this is far from being the case. But this is not enough. The various members in the institution also need to be have what I have called effective moral empowerment: the power to exercise the moral rights and fulfill the obligations, and the opportunity to interact with other members of the moral community in ways conducive to appropriate moral relations. In one and the same institution a right can be explicitly declared while the exercise of it, especially by the more vulnerable members, is systematically blocked, often without malice or awareness. As we have already noted, the different forms of subtle power at work are not easily recognized. Sometimes a simple "refusal to engage" is all that is needed, given the power relations. Before the requirements of membership in the moral community are properly incorporated into the functioning of any institution, the relationships between institutional members may need actively rebuilding. The default position of not doing so is in fact not "neutral," but, rather, one of disempowerment of the most vulnerable.

If we take seriously the implications of being a member of the moral community, then we must beware of aiming for an institution that runs very smoothly. An institution that is functioning well in a moral sense will have its share of hiccups and honest mistakes, but it will embody appropriate moral relations among its members. Indeed, for an institution to run well, it must avoid pretending to run perfectly. Paradoxically, one of the signals of a corrupt institution is an impossibly perfect public image, which in practice indicates the blocking of protests, the concealment of wrongs, the refusal to listen to input that would improve overall functioning, and similar suppression. It indicates, in fact, the effective disempowerment of its members and an oppressive mode of functioning, however unintended and habitual.

And respecting the kinds of relationships called for brings with it a bonus. In institutions where information is given, decisions are explained, comments are invited, dissent is expressed, protests are not blocked, and mistakes are rectified, full-blown, public protests are rare precisely because concerns can be raised at an early stage. This allows for misunderstandings to be corrected early, and for genuine oversights to be amended before too much harm is done, and within institutions far more harms and injustices occur because of a lack of awareness and understanding than through malice. It also fosters a more genuine form of trust, not because everyone will agree but because, if there is a disagreement, the person concerned will be the first to know. And if there *is* apparent agreement, it is far more likely to be genuine. In fact, if the requirements that stem from agent membership in the moral community are built into institutional relationships, and if the wider moral implications of the institution's goals and projects are explored, then fidelity to a specific code of ethics, a belief in the aims of the institution, loyalty to it and to its members, and a concern for its smooth and efficient functioning, can all thrive as sound and fruitful commitments. They have a legitimate importance precisely because they have no automatic priority over the demands of morality in the wider sense.

INSTITUTIONAL AGENTS

I will now look a little more closely at institutional involvement in wrongdoing. In the realm of person-to-person wrongs (where no institution is involved), adults with standard abilities are held accountable for their own actions. The only adults they can genuinely apologize for, for example, are themselves, although they can express regret at the wrongdoing of another adult. Apologizing, after all, is connected with reconciliation between the wrongdoer and the person wronged. If one adult seems to be apologizing for some other adult, we look for an underlying connection between the two, some relevant comembership in a collective or institution, however modest. We no longer have a simple person-to-person wrong.

A few collectives are very large, like the citizens of a populous state, or those affiliated to some religious faith. Comembership usually seems less significant, less correlated with any shared responsibility in such cases, but even here there have been instances where one member has apologized on behalf of earlier members. Some German citizens born after the Holocaust have apologized to Jewish survivors and the families of those killed, on behalf of the contributory acts of ordinary German citizens a generation earlier. But even if we stay with more manageable collectives, midsized institutions and smaller, the key issues still arise.

The first main question is, When does an act count as an institutional wrong? As a beginning, the phrase applies only when we are dealing with *institutional agents*, but this should not be oversimplified. In some cases acting as an institutional agent is a role that ends at a certain time of day. A salesperson who is rude and obstructive to elderly customers while working in a department store is acting in the role of agent of that store, but she is not acting in that role if she is rude and abusive to some elderly person on the way to the library. But with some less usual institutions, once a member, all of one's acts are in the role of institutional agent. If someone is a Roman Catholic priest, it is not just for certain hours a day. All of the person's acts are those of a priest, and so he may be held accountable, as a priest, for any act. In other cases of institutional membership it is less clear how continuous the agency is, but this is enough to alert us to oversimplifying here.

What is more crucial is that even when someone is clearly in an institutional role, some acts are more institutional than others. To explain why, we should note some basic things about institutions.

THE "RULES AND DECISIONS" OF AN INSTITUTION

Every institution is an organization to some degree. Typically there is a declaration of the institution's goals, and there are regulations about the proper functioning of its various parts, both in relation to each other and to things external to the institution. There will also be a series of specific major decisions reached by due institutional process. Within this set of goals, regulations about functioning, and specific major decisions, some items may require some act to be done or not done, others may explicitly permit some act. More developed institutions will capture all these things in writing. A less secure type of explicitness is to announce them orally on a regular basis.

In addition to these explicit items, there are often common practices and ways of doing things that are not made explicit, but because of their use through time, are well known and tacitly agreed upon. They can be ended at any time by explicit rules, but until that occurs, doing this or that over time, openly, and without institutional intervention, indicates a tacit institutional acceptance of the practice. There functions a *tacit rule of permission*.[11]

An institution's explicit declaration of goals, regulations about functioning, and specific major decisions, taken together with the institution's tacit rules of permission, constitute what I call *the rules and decisions* of the institution.

WRONGS MORE OR LESS INSTITUTIONAL

There are then two basic ways in which someone in the role of an institutional agent can be responsible for a serious moral wrong. First, the act may be consistent with a decision or with an explicit or tacit rule that is itself unacceptable morally. The rule or decision may either require or permit something seriously immoral, but in either case it fails morally. Here the wrong—or at least the potential for wrong—is embedded in some goal, process, practice, or decision of the institution, and in that sense the wrong is *institutionally sanctioned*.

The second way an institutional agent can be responsible for a wrong is by an immoral act that violates a rule that in itself presents no moral problem. Here the wrong is counter to some rule or decision of the institution, and so the wrong is *institutionally prohibited*.

When the German government made a major decision, making it illegal for Jews to own property, then a government official who confiscated a Jewish home by forcibly removing the family into a ghetto was committing an institutionally sanctioned wrong. When in a number of cities in occupied lands German soldiers made a practice of forcing all Jews to give way to them by making them step off the pavement into the gutter, this practice was openly performed without intervention from their military superiors. So it is fair to describe the German army as having a tacit rule of permission for this act. In some places it apparently became explicit after a time, but even with just a tacit rule, the wrong was again sanctioned. On the other hand if a bank employee embezzles money from a vulnerable client, this is institutionally prohibited.

So even when someone is clearly in an institutional role, some acts are more institutional than others. Morally speaking, institutionally sanctioned wrongs are more institutional than wrongs that are prohibited. Other things being equal, the latter are more the wrongs of individuals than of institutions.

Having set out the distinction above, there is a caveat. An institutionally prohibited wrong *can* still involve the institution as such, in four ways in particular.

The first is when the agent of the prohibited wrong is someone with an exceptional degree of responsibility or power within the institution, perhaps even a representative of the institution as a whole, like a prime minister, school principal, or the Pope. When such an agent commits a serious wrong that is institutionally prohibited, it seems to reflect more on the institution as a whole than when someone with far less responsibility commits a wrong.

Second, we may speak of institutional involvement if there is a rash of prohibited wrongs committed by many different institutional agents, since then the sheer numbers become relevant. In some places in Western countries in recent years, the number of Roman Catholic priests and lay brothers charged with multiple cases of sexual assault has led some to claim that the institution has some serious and systemic fault. If the number of agents involved is large enough, an institution may eventually be charged with being generally corrupt.

Third, the institution may be involved in having been biased or careless in placing or reviewing the individual in the institutional role. The more power that role has, the more scope there is for its abuse, and so the more care should be taken in selecting the person. No institution can be infallible, and there are limits on what can morally be done by way of choosing and supervising the institutional agent. Even so, given the nature of some roles, a great deal of care may be called for, and inadequate care constitutes a type of negligence.

The fourth common kind of involvement becomes possible once the prohibited wrong has occurred. Powerful agents in the institution may turn away from relevant evidence or from the victims' protest, either by not undertaking any investigation or by initiating a full-scale cover up, possibly involving retaliation on protesting victims or witnesses. Any of these kinds of involvement constitute a more or less serious type of complicity in the wrong.

INSTITUTIONAL APOLOGIES

In this final section of the chapter I will look at the incidents of institutional apologies that have begun to occur in recent years. When we consider the moral role of apologies as distinct from, for example, matters of financial compensation, we find that their importance is far greater than most nonvictims would think, and that importance stems directly from the underlying importance of the moral relationships involved. The issue, in fact, serves as a useful illustration of the central role played by those relationships, and reminds us how easily nonvictims in relatively powerful positions lose sight of them and their impact on the day-to-day lives of the oppressed. There has been work done on the emotional content in expressions of guilt and shame by institutional representatives (such as in *Fruits of Sorrow* by Elizabeth Spelman[12]), but in the following account I keep to the more basic questions about recognition of distorted relationships and the importance of acknowledging them.

Just as we ask if an individual is responsible for a wrong before acknowledging that her apology would be appropriate, so too we can ask if an institution is responsible for some wrong before agreeing that an apology is called for. This amounts to asking how institutional the wrong is. The more institutional the wrong, the more appropriate it is for apologies to be offered to the victims by an institutional representative, at some later time if necessary. Clearly this includes institutionally sanctioned wrongs generally recognized as such in society at large. In the case of institutionally prohibited wrongs, it applies if there is any significant institutional involvement, such as any of the four kinds mentioned above. These kinds of involvement differ in moral seriousness, but none is trivial.

The kinds of incidents I am referring to often involve what I call "representative apologies" in that the wrong was committed at an earlier time and the apologizer representing the institution was not personally involved. Consider the following four relevant cases: (1) The prime minister of Canada apologized to the Canadians of Japanese descent who were interned during the Second World War. (2) A representative of the Japanese government apologized to the Korean women who were "forcibly prostituted" to Japanese soldiers during that same war. (3) In France, some elderly concentration-camp survivors called for President Mitterand to apologize, in the name of France, for the wartime Vichy government's deportation of 76,000 French Jews to Nazi concentration camps. Only 2,600 survived. (4) In the Canadian Mount Cashel orphanage in Newfoundland, children were abused physically, sexually, and psychologically by several of the Catholic lay brothers running the place. There's some evidence that when complaints and cries for help eventually surfaced, the hierarchy of the Catholic Church rescued no one and dismissed no one. In later years the archbishop of the region offered an apology to the victims of this earlier abuse.

The importance of such apologies is something that should be addressed immediately, since it is no accident that powerful institutional members may consider the whole issue of apologizing to victims of earlier institutional wrongs a trivial matter, while the victims involved consider it very important indeed. The latter becomes increasingly clear from the newspaper and television coverage of relevant incidents. For example, a woman testifying at an inquiry into AIDS-infected blood given by the Canadian Red Cross in blood transfusions broke down when she said, "If only someone would say they were sorry." Canadians of Chinese descent recall the "Chinese head tax" paid only by immigrants from China decades ago. Not a few have written letters to the editors of various newspapers saying that for them, compensation is not the point; what matters is that they receive an apology. And every few weeks, there is coverage of another badly wronged victim making a powerful appeal for an institutional apology.

Significantly, those insisting on their importance tend to be far less powerful socially than those who have a dismissive attitude to the whole issue, since apologies matter first and foremost to the victims, and victims of institutional wrongs (at least, those without genuine redress) lack an appropriate level of power. If there is a danger in all this, it is that many academics (although by no means all) have had a privileged social status for most of their adult lives, and they may find it quite easy, therefore, to ignore the perspective of less powerful victims and the morally relevant issues that arise from that perspective.

These issues, however, are crucial when examining proper institutional functioning and the appropriate relationship between an institution and those it has wronged, and they should concern most especially those in powerful institutional roles. Not rarely, they are the only ones in a position to bring about any needed changes.

There has been some resistance to the idea of representative apologies, especially from powerful institutional agents not personally involved in the earlier wrong. For example, in Canada in the 1950s, the government moved seventeen Inuit families from Northern Quebec to a desolate location in the High Arctic. They were left in appalling conditions, having to survive the first winter in tents, and although promised the option of returning home if they wished, it seems that promise was broken.[13] A few years ago, Indian Affairs Minister Thomas Siddon and other officials rejected the call for an apology. Richard Van Loon, a top executive in the department, is reported to have said: "An apology implies we're apologizing for something that we did. Now there's nobody in the government that had anything to do with the relocation at the original time, so I think it might be more appropriate to say there'd be an expression of regret on behalf of the Canadian people."[14] (This position conflicts with a Canadian Human Rights Commission report that includes the recommendation that the government apologize for the hardship caused to the Inuit.) The officials are in fact denying that an institution, as distinct from individual agents within it, can be accountable in an ongoing way, and so are rejecting the call for representative apologies. (They are also denying the full role of the Canadian government in this case. It is extremely dubious how many of "the Canadian people" ever heard of the relocation until recently.)

On the other hand, I am claiming that since some wrongs *are* institutional, then if apologies are not offered at the time, there is a moral role to be played by representative apologies at a later time, especially if the institution is still in operation. Ideally the apology should come from the actual agents involved, but in practice this may not be feasible, especially if the wrong is well concealed or involves many agents committing some prohibited wrong or if the injustice is one not generally recognized in the society at the time, since then time passes before the wrong is finally acknowledged.

FOCUS ON CULPABILITY OR ON THE VICTIMS?

It may be objected that in some cases, although the acts were morally wrong, the institution was not culpable. Perhaps the wrongs were of a kind not generally recognized at the time. In some of the examples mentioned this distinction between a morally wrong act and a culpable agent is not crucial, because it would be unreasonable to claim an excusable lack of awareness with respect to the immorality of the act, such as the Vichy government's sending French Jews to German concentration camps. But there has been a general lack of awareness of other long-standing and serious wrongs, until well into this century. These include the oppression of ethnic minorities, the subjection of women, the domination of children, and the abuse of animals, especially where these various wrongs have taken a form not involving physical violence. Consequently there have been times and places when an institution could claim nonculpability as agent, even though the acts were seriously immoral. It would seem that institutional apologies, even by the actual agents, are not called for in such cases. The motive for setting aside apologies here is innocent, namely to spare the nonculpable agent embarrassment and humiliation if the wrongdoings were committed with an excusable lack of awareness.

Unfortunately, the result has often been to protect the feelings and reputations of powerful institutional agents, rather than acknowledge those wrongs and respond to the victims in appropriate ways. The most active forms of such protection may involve a deliberate cover-up, but there are other ways of suppressing reference to the wrong, involving complicitous silence or evasion, or acts of omission like refraining from investigating an injustice, or refusing to reconsider someone's role in the institution. When past acts of oppression must be mentioned, it is often with an appalling briskness. In the worst cases there is scant if any recognition of there being victims: the harm and misery they have endured is not acknowledged, there is no attempt to undo or minimize the harm, and the victims are expected not to refer to the wrongs and not to embarrass the institution, on pain of being shunned or worse. It is relatively easy for the less active kinds of involvement to be described in ways that seem to have no moral relevance. Perhaps it is a matter of being "too busy," or "not wanting to be rude," or "not wanting to go over the past." In fact, the less active forms of involvement may be altogether unconscious. None of this is rare, and it need not involve genuine malice. It is just a matter of focus. If the concern is for the sensibilities of nonculpable agents, then the hazards for the victims' situation may pass unnoted.

But I am suggesting that priority should be given to the victims and the injustice and harm inflicted on them, not to the culpability or otherwise of the institutional agents. If the rights of the victims conflict with the otherwise appropriate consideration for nonculpable agents, then I believe our obligations to the victims have the greater moral urgency.

If we look at the two categories of institutional wrongs set out earlier, one in particular includes cases of nonculpable agency: that of institutionally sanctioned wrongs. In Western countries, major institutions and influential professions—like the medical and legal professions, mainline Christian denominations, universities, governments, and more—have had long-standing, institutionally sanctioned rules, both explicit and tacit, that have excluded, marginalized, and denigrated ethnic minorities, women, homosexuals, the physically challenged, and others. Society at large has taken a very long time even to begin to recognize the serious wrongs involved, especially when these rules have not involved the use of physical force. This means that many of these wrongs have involved nonculpable institutional agents.

But even when the wrongs begin to change in status from institutionally sanctioned to prohibited, there seems to be a reluctance to approach the actual victims with an explicit acknowledgment of the wrong and a sincere and meaningful expression of regret for the harm and misery endured and for the derailment of their life's path so often involved. Should we call this an apology? That depends on whether it is conceptually possible to apologize for a genuine wrongdoing that, however, one was nonculpably unaware of at the time. Rather than be sidetracked by this, I will speak here of a public expression of sincere regret, made to the victims. If this is the better phrase, then it is because of the nonculpability of the original insitutional agents rather than because more recent insitutional agents (not involved in the original wrong) are the ones now representing the institution.

So far, however, the relevant professional associations, universities, governments, and churches have tended not to express regret to the various groups of people for the misery and harm caused in such situations. Only a few such instances have been referred to in the public media. For example, a Canadian representative of a Christian denomination has addressed native peoples who were subjected to the sanctioned domination and cultural obliteration committed in the name of "missionary work." (The representative actually used the terminology of "an apology," but it is the closest case I know of where there was, at the relevant time, considerable societal unawareness about many of the wrongs involved.) No doubt there have been a few other cases of publicly expressed regrets where the original institutional agents were nonculpable, but it is significant that during the few years of collecting reported examples, only this one in a fairly large collection involved santioned wrongs committed with an excusable lack of awareness. Nearly all the actual cases involved institutional representatives apologizing (rather than expressing regrets) for earlier moral wrongs that were recognizably wrongs, yet sanctioned by the institution. For example, the German government has apologized for the earlier sanctioned wrongs against the Jews, but these wrongs hardly qualify as being committed nonculpably. I did not hear reported one analogous act directed to homosexuals, women, or the physically disabled, for example. This apparent trend may be misleading, since the practice of public institutional apologies and expressions of regret is in its early stages, but I predict that it will be sustained by an inappropriate emphasis on the nonculpability of the agents.

WHY EXPRESSIONS OF REGRET ARE IMPORTANT

I believe that public expressions of regret are appropriate in such cases. Societies that have any hope for them at all are in the process of growing in moral awareness. Obviously this is desirable, but it brings with it the considerable pain that occurs when we recognize as a wrong something we have performed or supported until then. Anyone who takes seriously the human task of growing in moral awareness is facing that kind of pain, and those in positions of power are likely at times to realize that their being previously unaware has resulted in harm and injustice of one kind or another. Someone who cannot face this fact honestly is rather too dangerous to place in a position of power, since when the time comes, that person will deny or trivialize what has happened to the victims, and abandon them to a fate not of their making. All too often the familiar cry of "what's done is done" is true not as a factual report, but only as an institutional decision about how victims are to be treated.

Serious injustice matters more than the embarrassment of realizing that we are not morally perfect or that we took a long time to become aware. In fact the only people who are free from this kind of painful realization are those who cannot or will not be open minded and increasingly perceptive about previously unrecognized wrongs. The price paid for such deceptive psychological comfort is far too high, and it is a price paid mainly by the victims.

There are other related reasons for public expressions of regret. For one thing, the sheer amount of injustice and suffering resulting from nonculpably committed, institutionally sanctioned wrongs is immense. The vast number of victims whose lives have been distorted or derailed gives rise to more not less moral urgency for the acknowledgment of the wrong and for representative expressions of regret.

Also, since these expressions are public to some degree or other, they, like the protests of victims, draw attention to the wrong and further the growing societal awareness of others like it. They can also serve to encourage other institutions to be similarly responsive.

Moving back now to the whole range of cases where apologies (or regrets) are appropriate, there is a final reason why the apologies are more important than first appears, whether the wrongs were blatant or unrecognized. Nonvictims of good will often find it much easier to see the importance of compensation than of apologies, which is understandable given that compensation typically involves very tangible sorts of goods (like money). But it is not unusual for victims of institutional wrongs to declare that an apology is at least as important and, not rarely, more important, than financial compensation. This, I suggest, is not to be reduced to simply a psychological benefit to the victims, however legitimate, but rather, it is because the offering of apologies plays a vital role in amending the relationships that have become seriously distorted, something of particular interest to us in this work.

In particular, it often plays a crucial role in amending the relationship between the *victims and the institution*, between the *victims and the moral community at large*, and between the *victims and their local community*. All three enter into the points below, but it can be said immediately that depending on the importance of the institution in the lives of the victims, and depending on how badly the relationship with the community at large has been damaged, amending these relationships can be essential to the rebuilding of lives sometimes devastated by institutional wrongs.

Apologies or expressions of regret are important in the process of reconciliation between victims and institutions. Victims of extensive or cumulative injustice committed without awareness find no special comfort in just hearing the explanation that it was not explicitly intended, but rather arose out of the sincere belief that they were literally the property of their parents, or that they were meant to be subservient to whites, or meant to be the handmaids of husbands, or were not able to learn anything because they were deaf. Actual victims of such institutionally enacted attitudes and beliefs not surprisingly tend to be alienated from those institutions. This alienation and isolation can be made even greater if the victims try to convey the full dimensions of the harm and misery involved. They are likely to have a very difficult time of it, far more so than in the case of well-recognized wrongs, since the wrongs here are but newly acknowledged as a type of wrong. Also, these wrongs are not randomly distributed throughout society. In particular, they do not usually fall to the lot of the privileged members of society, which again makes it very difficult to convey to powerful institutional representatives just what is involved. This is especially so in the case of serious but nontangible kinds of harm, like moral abandonment, or the kinds of second-order suppression I have referred to as victim oppression.

Reconciliation with an agent of some wrong involves the building of a new and more appropriate relationship, often to replace one that has become badly flawed. It does not have to involve forgiveness in the literal sense: it need not involve one party's being morally culpable. Relationships can become badly distorted without that, and prime candidates are the relationships between the recipients of extensive injustice and the institutions that are nonculpably responsible. The irony is that groups of victims have sometimes shown themselves far more willing than the relevant institutions to restore proper relationships. Some institutions have resolutely refused to "forgive" their actual victims, opting instead for the morally inadequate response of focusing solely on the next generation of the affected groups and beginning to treat those individual members more fairly.

In the ordinary run of things, acts that sustain the moral empowerment of individuals with respect to the basic rights and obligations set out earlier help to establish the proper moral relationships, at least, when the acts are done with the right kind of attitude. But when things have gone badly wrong already, the relationships are being constructed not on a neutral foundation, but on one that is distorted. This is the situation for actual victims of institutional wrongs, and we owe it to the victims to jump start the reconstruction of relationships. Representative apologies or expressions of regret are, among other things, just such an initiative.

Apologies are in any case owed to the victims as members of the moral community. Once a significant wrong is perceived, for institutional representatives to walk away from the victims in silence is to exhibit a serious moral contempt for them. They are being accorded a kind of third-rate membership in the moral community, and again, if we listen to victims who are calling for an institutional apology, then this final expression of moral contempt can be as devastating, sometimes more devastating, than the original wrong.

Silence in the case of sanctioned wrongs with nonculpable institutional agents is especially pernicious since the victims are at the receiving end of systematic oppression rather than isolated acts of malice or negligence, so their experience of having an inferior status within the moral community is all too extensive already. The acknowledgment of and regret for the institutional wrongs involved is a kind of long overdue, public declaration of their proper status within the moral community.

If we move now to the relationship between the victims and their local community, institutional apologies often play an important role in re-establishing the public standing of the victims, and in validating them as honest and accurate recounters of events. For example, there have been cases where children and teens who were sexually or physically abused in orphanages or reform schools run by Christian organizations have acquired general credibility in the community at large only as adults, and only when the institutions involved finally admitted and apologized for the abuse. Those who before this time spoke out about their abuse often found themselves shunned as either a committed liar or mentally confused. Those who felt they had to keep silent about something so life-altering often found themselves dismissed as irrationally secretive, antisocial, and strange. Relationships with others in their local community, even sometimes with relatives, often began to be appropriately changed only when the institution responsible admitted and apologized for the wrong in some relatively public fashion.

In addition to the various reasons already offered here for the importance of institutional apologies, it is worth remembering that offering apologies can be a striking, even moving, expression of an institution's moral integrity. In Western societies in these times we have all but forgotten the fact that an act of apology, in the right circumstances, is an act of courage, and reflects moral strength, not weakness.

SINCERITY AND INTENTIONS FOR THE FUTURE

To really be the refreshing change they seem to be, the acts of apology or expressions of regret need to meet some basic conditions of moral soundness. Institutions offering apologies solely because they have been found out in a previously concealed wrong usually do not meet these conditions. I will look particularly at the matter of "sincerity."

In a person-to-person apology, simply saying the right words may deceive the victim and bring comfort, but it does not constitute a genuine apology if sincerity is lacking. An apology can greatly contribute to amending an unsound relationship, but for the relationship to be genuinely as it should be, the person's attitude is crucial, especially her condemnation of the wrong, and remorse for her part in it and for the resulting harm. Also, sincerity is naturally associated with certain actions, such as trying to undo the harm so far as possible, forming the intention not to repeat the wrong in the future, and following through on that intention.

If we move to someone apologizing on behalf of an institution and ask what the parallel point would be, it is easy to oversimplify. Of course the apologizer needs to be sincere so far as he can be, given that ex hypothesi he was not involved in the original wrongdoing and so cannot regret his role in it. He can sincerely condemn the wrong, regret that it occurred, and that it caused harm. This much is analogous to a truly individual wrong, but this sincerity on the part of the representative apologizer is not enough.

The problem occurs when we speak of the intention not to repeat the wrong in the future and ask what this could translate into in the case of an institution. We do not mean simply the intention of the representative apologizer. An institution has many members, many separate wills, and all of its rules and decisions. So what is the closest this conglomeration can come to having "sincere intentions" for the future? The answer depends on the nature of the institutional wrong, and on the formal and practical measures most likely to prevent the wrong in the future. Let's look at a small sample of options.

(a) For *institutionally sanctioned wrongs*, what is needed to prevent further instances seems straightfoward: an explicit prohibition. It may not be easy to bring this about, but it does seem clear that this is the remedy.

It is true that this is the formal correction of an institutionally sanctioned wrong, and sometimes no more is needed. If a department store charges women for basic alterations to suits they buy but does not charge men, then explicitly prohibiting charging women should be enough. Unless there is widespread corruption among the institutional members, violations of this new rule are easily established and so it can be easily enforced.

But it is naive to think that such formal correction alone is always sufficient to effect real change. Many countries have all kinds of laws prohibiting acts that are still routinely performed. This is particularly true where long-standing bias, rather than explicit and malicious intent, is at work. Hundreds of people who are superbly qualified for the employment they apply for are denied it, because they are black, or older than most applicants, or in a wheelchair (all illegal criteria for selection in Canada, for example). But given what is involved in many hiring processes, there is in practice rarely any effective recourse. At the moment what many of these laws really amount to is the warning that if you are not going to hire someone because he/she is black, or older, or in a wheelchair, don't be foolish enough to say it is because he/she is black, or older, or in a wheelchair. If that caution is heeded, then ninety-nine times out of a hundred, an institution will be invulnerable.

Biased and prejudiced acts are actually harder to prohibit successfully than outright malicious acts, since so many of the former are habit driven. Visibility becomes even more of a problem if the bias and prejudice result in a series of acts of *omission*. Adding to the difficulty is the fact that people who are full of good will and genuinely committed to upholding the prohibition often find themselves defeated. They may not understand how the bias works (such as, often via the cumulative blocking effect of a long series of apparently unimportant acts). Or they may know intellectually, but lack the perceptual skills to spot the relevant acts when they actually occur.

For these kinds of reasons, sincerity about prohibiting some previously sanctioned wrongs involves not only formal correction, but also other practical measures. Suggestions have included educational programs, action on equity measures, and more. I will not try to assess them here. Too much is involved. The only point for this dicussion is that sometimes practical measures of some kind are not frills, but part of a sincere commitment to the new prohibition.

(b) For *institutional involvement in prohibited wrongs*, what is called for depends on the nature of the involvement. If the school principal has for years changed the exam grades for pupils who pay for it, then the principal should be removed from employment within the teaching profession. If many institutional members are seriously corrupt so that many prohibited wrongs are being committed, then those members not involved may need to call upon some form of power external to the institution before the situation can change. If an institution has been negligent in the placing or fair supervising of an institutional agent, then the procedures need either following more closely or revising.

This brings us to perhaps the most prevalent form of institutional involvement: the turning away from evidence that something is wrong or from protests about the wrong. In its worst form it involves actively organizing a cover-up and retaliation on those protesting. In its less blatant forms it involves the less active ways of turning away from "unpleasantness." The one serious reservation I have about actual representative apologies reported so far is that they tend not to include apologies for this kind of involvement even when it is crystal clear that it was a major part of the problem.

If the prohibited wrong is one generally recognized in society as immoral, and yet there are a number of victims over a period of months or even years, then something is very wrong with the relationship between the powerful members of that institution and the victims. Either the victims protested and were ignored, or were summarily dismissed as liars, or suffered relatiation or harassment, or the victims were too intimidated to protest, or were trapped in an isolated and enclosed environment with no one to protest to, or something else was terribly wrong. When the wrong involves some such matter, a representative apology can be taken as sincere only if the institution gets down to work on how to build a morally appropriate relationship between its powerful members and whoever the victims are (including those who are already victims, as well as the next generation of potential victims). That relationship will be one where the actual and potential victims genuinely can protest serious wrongs and have their protests considered fairly and with an open mind. For some institutions, such as some very traditional Christian institutions, that would involve a radical change in how they actually function.

THE JOY OF IMPERFECT INSTITUTIONS

In recent years there have been reported in the public media many instances of blatant institutional wrongs that have been formerly concealed. In addition, we have begun to understand that there is far more involved in an institution's behaving justly than most people realized forty or even twenty years ago. Accidental oversights and even a society-wide lack of awareness account for far more injustices and wrongs than do malice or indifference.

No institution can be perfect, but the difference between an imperfect institution and one that is corrupt lies mainly in how it handles its imperfections. Powerful institutional agents usually have a personal stake in the institution's "looking good," so it is no trivial task to create or sustain a basically sound mode of functioning. The challenge is to create institutions unafraid of being just. It involves institutional agents who are at ease with the fact that fresh moral insights bring with them painful times, and it means being honest about institutional wrongs, both obvious wrongs and those where there was a reasonable lack of awareness at the time. It calls for institutional agents who care about justice, however belated, who are committed to restoring morally appropriate relationships, and who resist placing a false public image ahead of either. In such commitments we find the only secure buttress against arrogance, corrupt power, and the marginalization of an institution's victims.

But these commitments cannot reasonably be sustained unless all members of the institution take a more courageous approach to the obligations that attach to membership in the moral community. As already stated in this chapter, serious injustice and the resulting distorted relationships matter more than the embarrassment that nonculpable agents experience when some wrong is eventually recognized. Expressions of regret are due, and the relationships need to be rebuilt. But this is quite compatible with claiming that, in certain circumstances, the less powerful have a prima facie obligation to take their concerns to the contributing agent first (and preferably early). Much earlier in the work I argued that cilivized oppression can be reduced only if it is seen as a mutual endeavor actively involving both the more powerful and the more vulnerable.

In such mutually supportive commitments we find what I call the joy of imperfect institutions—institutions regretful but honest about their lack of perfection. Basically sound functioning is quite compatible with institutional imperfection. In fact, anyone who ties sound functioning to perfection has no viable concept to work with. Maintaining the integrity of the moral community within a midsized institution makes serious demands of all the members, but the demands are realistic. Many institutions fail, and not a few are heading in well intentioned but misguided directions (trying to amend the situation by transferring abusive power from one group to another, for example). But it is only when the nature of civilized oppression is carefully examined that we can undertake a more focused approach to it in institutionalized settings.

IN RETROSPECT

This chapter has made a brief foray into the world of our everday institutions. There we find tangible locations for active involvement in securing morally sound relationships. Since we are now at the end of the work, it is time to look back on how we reached this point. We perceive more when we understand better, and this inquiry has led from surface features of social life to the structure of the moral community.

The analysis began with familiar social situations involving no violence, and no physical or legal coercion. By exploring some of these situations, we came to discern inconspicuous power relations and subtle mechanisms of control, and to understand why they are so commonly invisible to those involved. The analysis required the development of relevant concepts, such as relationship power in its various forms, and then at the level of moral assessment, the concepts of moral subordination and moral abandonment. These structures of exclusion and subordination led to the insight that at the heart of civilized oppression lies morally inappropriate relationships rather than tangible harms.

Reflection on what is wrong with oppressive relationships led to an understanding of their pervasive importance: they involve moral rights and obligations that are basic in a special way. These are rights and obligations that belong simply to agent membership in the moral community, and they therefore hold at a level more fundamental than the levels where most differences in substantive moral views appear. The analysis of oppressive relationships and the account of their moral inappropriateness—two of the aims set out at the beginning of this work—together support the other main aim, namely, to make civilized oppression more visible. But we need not view it as an inevitable part of everyday life. The subtle nature of such oppression renders it neither incomprehensible nor permanently beyond remedy.

NOTES

1. Conrad G. Brunk, "Professionalism and Responsibility in the Technological Society," in *Business Ethics in Canada*, 2d ed., ed. Deborah C. Poff and Wilfrid J. Waluchow (Scarborough, Ontario: Prentice-Hall, 1991), 127.

2. Brunk, 127.

3. Brunk, 133.

4. Beth Savan, "Beyond Professional Ethics: Issues and Agendas," in *Business Ethics in Canada*, 2d ed., ed. Deborah C. Poff and Wilfrid J. Waluchow (Scarborough, Ontario: Prentice-Hall, 1991), 172.

5. Brunk, 123.

6. Brunk, 124.

7. *Hansard's Parliamentary Debates*, Second Series, vol. 24, 999; House of Commons, May 24, 1830 (London: H.M. Stationery Office, 1830).

8. H. R. Smith and Archie B. Carroll, "Organizational Ethics: A Stacked Deck," in *Business Ethics in Canada*, 2d ed., ed. Deborah C. Poff and Wilfrid J. Waluchow (Scarborough, Ontario: Prentice-Hall, 1991), 233.

9. Smith and Carroll, 233.

10. E.g., Alex Michalos, "Moral Responsibility in Business," in *Business Ethics in Canada*, 2d ed., ed. Deborah C. Poff and Wilfrid J. Waluchow (Scarborough, Ontario: Prentice-Hall, 1991); Alex Michalos, "The Loyal Agent's Argument," in Poff and Waluchow, 2d ed.; Frederick Bird and Jeffrey Gandz, *Good Management: Business Ethics in Action* (Scarborough, Ontario: Prentice-Hall, 1991), especially chapter 9, "Designing Ethically Responsible Organizations."

11. Sometimes there is a period when it is unclear if the practice has moved from being merely accepted to being expected or required. This can happen when the practice is uniformly followed, so there are no visible exceptions. This can leave it unclear whether exceptions would be acceptable or not. But for simplicity, I refer only to tacit *rules of permission* and not to the stronger idea of tacit rules *requiring* this or that. This type of confusion should not arise with well articulated, explicit regulations.

12. Elizabeth Spelman, *Fruits of Sorrow* (Boston: Beacon Press, 1997), 100–109.

13. It has also been claimed that one motive for the relocation of the Inuit was not humanitarian (e.g., the scarcity of game in the original location), but a way of asserting Canadian sovereignty in the High Arctic. For a full and authoritative account of the whole episode see Royal Commission on Aboriginal Peoples, *The High Arctic Relocation: A Report on the 1953–55 Relocation* (Ottawa: Supply and Services, 1994).

14. Reported in *Vancouver Sun* [Canadian newspaper], 16 January 1992, A3.

Works Cited

Ackerman, Bruce A. *Social Justice in the Liberal State*. New Haven, Conn.: Yale University Press, 1980.

Andre, Judith. "Power, Oppression and Gender." *Social Theory and Practice* 11, no. 1 (Spring 1985): 107–22.

Arendt, Hannah. "The Deputy: Guilt by Silence?" In *Amor Mundi*, edited by James W. Bernauer. Dordrecht: Martinus Nijhoff, 1987.

Bartky, Sandra Lee. *Femininity and Domination*. New York: Routledge, 1990.

Bergmann, Merrie. "How Many Feminists Does It Take to Make a Joke? Sexist Humor and What's Wrong with It." *Hypatia* 1, no. 1 (Spring 1986): 63–82.

Bergson, Henri. *Laughter: An Essay on the Meaning of the Comic*, trans. C. Brereton and F. Rothwell. London: Macmillan, 1911.

Bird, Frederick, and Jeffrey Gandz. *Good Management: Business Ethics in Action*. Scarborough, Ontario: Prentice-Hall, 1991.

Boxill, Bernard E. "Self-Respect and Protest." *Philosophy and Public Affairs* 6, no. 4 (Fall 1976): 58–69.

Bradney, Pamela. "The Joking Relationship in Industry." *Human Relations* 10, no. 2 (May 1957): 179–87.

Brison, Susan J. "Surviving Sexual Violence." *Journal of Social Philosophy* 24, no. 1 (Spring 1993): 5–22.

Brunk, Conrad G. "Professionalism and Responsibility in the Technological Society." In *Business Ethics in Canada*, 2d ed., edited by Deborah C. Poff and Wilfrid J. Waluchow. Scarborough, Ontario: Prentice-Hall, 1991.

Calhoun, Cheshire. "Responsibility and Reproach." *Ethics* 99, no. 2 (January 1989): 389–406.

Chesterfield, Fourth Earl of. *Letters of Philip Dormer Stanhope, Earl of Chesterfield, with The Characters*, vol. I, edited by John Bradshaw. London: George Allen & Unwin, 1892.

Colby, Frank Moore. *Imaginary Obligations*. New York: Dodd, Mead, 1904.

Coser, Rose L. "Some Social Functions of Laughter." *Human Relations* 12, no. 2 (May 1959): 171–82.

———. "Laughter among Colleagues." *Psychiatry* 23, no. 1 (February 1960): 81–89.

Darwall, Stephen. "Two Kinds of Respect." *Ethics* 88, no. 1 (October 1977): 36–49.

de Sousa, Ronald. *The Rationality of Emotion.* Cambridge, Mass.: MIT Press, 1987.

Dillon, Robin S. "Toward a Feminist Conception of Self-Respect." *Hypatia* 7, no. 1 (Winter 1992): 52–69.

Feinberg, Joel. *Harm to Others.* New York: Oxford University Press, 1984.

Frye, Marilyn. *The Politics of Reality: Essays in Feminist Theory.* Freedom, California: Crossing Press, 1983.

Galston, William A. *Justice and the Human Good.* Chicago: University of Chicago Press, 1980.

Goldsmith, Oliver. "The Deserted Village." In *The Poetical Works of Goldsmith, Collins, and T. Warton,* edited by George Gilfillan. Edinburgh: James Nichol, 1854.

———. *The Vicar of Wakefield,* edited by Ernest Rhys. London: Walter Scott Ltd., 1889.

Hansard's Parliamentary Debates, Second Series, vol. 24, House of Commons. London: H.M. Stationery Office, 1830.

Harvey, J. "Forgiving as an Obligation of the Moral Life." *International Journal of Moral and Social Studies* 8, no. 3 (Autumn 1993): 211–22.

Hill, Thomas E. "Symbolic Protest and Calculated Silence." In *Autonomy and Self-Respect.* Cambridge: Cambridge University Press, 1991.

Hobbes, Thomas. *Leviathan,* edited by C. B. MacPherson. Harmondsworth, England: Penguin, 1968.

Illingworth, Patricia M. L. "Explaining without Blaming the Victim." *Journal of Social Philosophy* 21, no. 2–3 (Fall/Winter 1990): 117–26.

Kant, Immanuel. *Lectures on Ethics,* trans. Louis Infield. New York: Harper & Row, 1963.

———. *The Metaphysics of Morals,* trans. Mary Gregor. Cambridge: Cambridge University Press, 1991.

Kellenberger, J. *Relationship Morality.* University Park, Penn.: Pennsylvania State University Press, 1995.

Koggel, Christine M. *Perspectives on Equality.* Lanham, Md.: Rowman & Littlefield, 1998.

Lewontin, R. C. "Women Versus the Biologists." *The New York Review of Books,* 7 April 1994: 31–35.

Lyons, David. *Forms and Limits of Utilitarianism.* London: Oxford University Press, 1965.

McGary, Howard. "Forgiveness." *American Philosophical Quarterly* 26, no. 4 (October 1989): 343–51.

Michalos, Alex. "Moral Responsibility in Business." In *Business Ethics in Canada,* 2d ed., edited by Deborah C. Poff and Wilfrid J. Waluchow. Scarborough, Ontario: Prentice-Hall, 1991.

———. "The Loyal Agent's Argument." In *Business Ethics in Canada,* 2d ed., edited by Deborah C. Poff and Wilfrid J. Waluchow. Scarborough, Ontario: Prentice-Hall, 1991.

Mikes, George. *Humour in Memoriam.* London: Routledge & Kegan Paul, 1970.

Miller, David. *Social Justice.* Oxford: Clarendon Press, 1976.

Morreall, John. *Taking Laughter Seriously.* Albany, N.Y.: State University of New York Press, 1983.

————, ed. *The Philosophy of Laughter and Humor*. Albany, N.Y.: State University of New York Press, 1987.

Morris, Herbert. *On Guilt and Innocence*. Berkeley, Calif.: University of California Press, 1976.

Plato. *The Republic*, trans. F. M. Cornford. London: Oxford University Press, 1945.

Rawls, John. *A Theory of Justice*. Cambridge, Mass.: Harvard University Press, 1971.

Richards, Norvin. "Forgiveness." *Ethics* 99, no. 1 (October 1988): 77–97.

Royal Commission on Aboriginal Peoples. *The High Arctic Relocation: A Report on the 1953–55 Relocation*. Ottawa: Supply and Services, 1994.

Russell, Diana E. H. *The Politics of Rape*. New York: Stein & Day, 1975.

————. *Sexual Exploitation*. Beverly Hills, Calif.: Sage Publications, 1984.

Ryan, William. *Blaming the Victim*, rev. ed. New York: Vintage Books, 1976.

Savan, Beth. "Beyond Professional Ethics: Issues and Agendas." In *Business Ethics in Canada*, 2d ed., edited by Deborah C. Poff and Wilfrid J. Waluchow. Scarborough, Ontario: Prentice-Hall, 1991.

Sheridan, Richard Brinsley. Quoted in *The New Dictionary of Thoughts*, originally compiled by Tryon Edwards, rev. and enlarged by C. N. Catrevas, Jonathan Edwards, and Ralph Emerson Browns. Garden City, N.Y.: Standard Book Co., 1957.

Smith, H. R., and Archie B. Carroll. "Organizational Ethics: A Stacked Deck." In *Business Ethics in Canada*, 2d ed., edited by Deborah C. Poff and Wilfrid J. Waluchow. Scarborough, Ontario: Prentice-Hall, 1991.

Spelman, Elizabeth. *Fruits of Sorrow*. Boston: Beacon Press, 1997.

Szawarski, Zbigniew. "Dignity and Responsibility." *Dialectics and Humanism* 13, no. 2–3 (Spring/Summer 1986): 193–205.

Thomas, Laurence. *Living Morally*. Philadelphia: Temple University Press, 1989.

————. "Moral Deference." *The Philosophical Forum* 24, no. 1–3 (Fall/Spring 1992–93): 233–250.

————. "Self-Respect: Theory and Practice." In *Philosophy Born of Struggle: Anthology of Afro-American Philosophy from 1917*, edited by Leonard Harris. Dubuque, Iowa: Kendall/Hunt, 1983.

————. *Vessels of Evil: American Slavery and the Holocaust*. Philadelphia: Temple University Press, 1993.

Vancouver Sun [Canadian newspaper], 16 January 1992; 5 December 1992; 20 February 1993.

Vlastos, Gregory. "Justice and Equality." In *Social Justice*, edited by Richard Brandt. Englewood Cliffs, N.J.: Prentice-Hall, 1962.

Walker, Margaret Urban. *Moral Understandings*. New York: Routledge, 1998.

Wartenberg, Thomas E. *The Forms of Power*. Philadelphia: Temple University Press, 1990.

Wendell, Susan. "Oppression and Victimization: Choice and Responsibility." *Hypatia* 5, no. 3 (Fall 1990): 15–46.

Wiesstein, Naomi. "Why We Aren't Laughing Any More." *Ms.* 2 (November 1973): 49–51 & 88–90.

Wolgast, Elizabeth H. *The Grammar of Justice*. Ithaca, N.Y.: Cornell University Press, 1987.

Young, Iris Marion. *Justice and the Politics of Difference*. Princeton, N.J.: Princeton University Press, 1990.

Index

151

INDEX OF AUTHOR'S ILLUSTRATIVE EXAMPLES

About the Author

J. Harvey is an associate professor of philosophy at the University of Guelph, Ontario, and has a doctorate from the University of British Columbia. Harvey has published on a variety of issues about the place in moral theory of moral relationships, both personal and institutional, in such journals as the *Journal of Social Philosophy*, *The Journal of Value Inquiry*, the *International Journal of Moral and Social Studies*, and the *Canadian Journal of Philosophy*. Harvey's current work pursues further theoretical implications of the findings in this book.